A Chair for Pope Francis

A Collection of Designs for the Papal Sanctuary Charrette

A Chair for Pope Francis

A Collection of Designs for the Papal Sanctuary Charrette

Edited by Patricia Andrasik

With the assistance of Daniel Ruck

The School of Architecture and Planning

The Catholic University of America Press

Washington, DC

Distributed for the School of Architecture by the Catholic University of America Press

The paper used in this publication meets the minimum requirements of American National Standards for Information Science—Permanence of Paper for Printed Library materials, ANSI Z39.48-1984.

∞

Cataloging-in-Publication Data available from the Library of Congress
ISBN 978-1-329-70119-9

Foreword by His Eminence Cardinal Donald Wuerl Archbishop of Washington

When our Holy Father, Pope Francis, stepped out onto the refashioned East Portico of the Basilica of the National Shrine of the Immaculate Conception to celebrate the Canonization Mass of the then-Blessed Junípero Serra, he opened a new chapter in the long story of the Church in the United States. Here was the first pope to come from the New World, who was about to celebrate a canonization for the first time ever in the United States, of a humble Franciscan priest who brought the Faith to a significant portion of our nation. How fitting that this event taking place at the Basilica and on the grounds of The Catholic University of America would also reflect the vitality, genius and skills of so many of this generation of "young people" who were a part of that glorious day. The altar furniture for that Canonization Mass, which now graces the interior of the Basilica, was created and designed by students of the School of Architecture and Planning of The Catholic University of America and executed by a team of skilled craftsmen. This book tells the story of that work as well as of the efforts of those students who created other entries in the altar furnishing design competition.

Just as the great evangelizer Saint Junípero Serra O.F.M. devoted his life to spreading the word of Jesus Christ and to meeting the physical and spiritual welfare of the native population, the Successor of Peter visited the United States to share the joy of the Gospel and to encourage us all to walk with him as missionary disciples to proclaim the merciful love of God. The canonization of Saint Junípero was a significant and historic act, and it gave me great joy to know that the occasion was also one where the many talents of the student body at Catholic University shined forth.

Throughout the ages, artists have continuously joined their talents to their Catholic faith in service to the Church's mission of bringing to others an encounter with the saving love of Jesus Christ. In a particular way, men and women have sought to use their talents for the sublime purpose of making manifest the Kingdom of God through the mediums of stone, wood, metal and cloth in service to the liturgy.

Every piece of furniture on the altar bears significance and meaning, and the union of faith and architectural design for building furniture in support of the holiest of actions – the Mass – has a long and honored past. The opportunity to give form and function to the practice of our faith has led many to labor extremely hard, and sometimes without remuneration toward this blessed purpose. Often, these men and women spent years giving exclusive attention to these works of sacred art which they dedicated in their hearts and minds to the Greater Glory of God – Ad Majorem Dei Gloriam, a phrase we know as the motto of the Pope's own Society of Jesus.

The number of artists and architects who over the centuries have labored for God's glory through the gifts he gave each of them are not inconsiderable. Added to this fraternity of artistic missionaries are undoubtedly those students of Catholic University who offered designs for the papal altar and furniture for this historic Canonization Mass. The fact that they labored over designs to mark our Holy Father's visit after already completing studies and designs for their final academic projects is a testimony to their love for the Church.

Such generosity of talent and spirit as has poured forth here from the students at the School of Architecture and Planning is something we can all be grateful for. The effort put into this endeavor, and the creativity, beauty and thought that went into each of the submitted designs are visible signs of God's grace at work among us. The dedication of everyone involved also reminds us that, in whatever we do, we do it for the glory of God.

Dedicatory Epistle

To Pope Francis

To Our Holy Father, Pope Francis, a man chosen by God to shepherd His sheep to good pasture. Your mission has pervaded our modern world with His insight and shed light in the darkness. The impact of your mission is present in this publication, a compilation of works which constitute the official student entries for the Papal Sanctuary Charrette Competition.

A design solution was required for the furniture that would be constructed for your visit to the Basilica of the National Shrine of the Immaculate Conception at The Catholic University of America in Washington, DC on September 23, 2015. We thought that a 'charrette', an intensive collaborative design effort to create a project based on integrative ideas, would be the perfect platform to facilitate this competitive design endeavor.

The ambitions, challenges, successes and accomplishments of an interdisciplinary student body of The Catholic University of America depicted in this book are offered to you as small gifts of effort entwining theology, technology and sustainability into design.

Yours very truly,
The Students of The Catholic University of America

Acknowledgements

I would like to take this opportunity to gratefully acknowledge His Eminence **Cardinal Donald Wuerl**, *Archbishop of Washington, for his leadership in instituting Pope Francis' visit to The Catholic University of America, along with the initiative of the Most Reverend* **Barry C. Knestout**, *Vicar General and Moderator of the Curia of the Archdiocese of Washington DC, and Reverend Monsignor* **Walter R. Rossi**, *Rector of the Basilica of the National Shrine of the Immaculate Conception, for inviting the School of Architecture and Planning at our institution to help develop and administer the Papal Sanctuary Charrette Competition that made this collection of works possible. In particular, I would like to recognize their generosity in offering such high caliber awards to our students and the patience and sincere interest they and the other judging members exhibited when hearing each team's presentation during the final design jury.*

The success of the Competition would not have been possible without the support of **John Garvey**, *President of The Catholic University of America, of* **Frank Persico**, *President Garvey's Chief of Staff, and of* **Randall Ott**, *Dean of the School of Architecture and Planning, who together hosted and successfully facilitated this event despite the confluence of finals and graduation week.*

Deserving of special mention are **Professors Ann Cederna** *and* **Hollee Becker** *at the School of Architecture and Planning, who were faculty coordinators for the event. Through attention to myriad details, they made this event appear effortless.*

A specific recognition is deserving for the efforts of **ALL the teams** *featured herein. In addition to the projects designed by these student entrants, I would like to formally recognize a few students who have been instrumental in producing this publication:* **Ariadne Cerritelli** *(M.Arch student), who dedicated the last week of her summer to establish the preliminary layout of the publication,* **Elizabeth Bowlen** *(MSSD student), who transcribed text from the submissions, and* **Daniel R. Ruck** *(M.Arch and MSSD student), who spent three months in coordinating the edits and graphic design and who persisted in picking up redlines and adjustments through our Christmas break to make the completion of this book possible.*

Image provided by Chas Winebrenner and Andrew Anderson

TABLE OF CONTENTS

Editor's Preface

This book was assembled to present the profound interplay of theological, technological and environmental comprehension and interpretation present in, and the circumstances of the teams' processes leading to, the designs submitted by the students of The Catholic University School of Architecture and Planning for the Papal Sanctuary Charrette Competition.

As most architectural professionals understand, certain factors are anticipated in creating built work, including furniture. One of these is depth of concept, or a main idea which compels the design. The level of interaction between art and science as the design is developed is also an important consideration. In some cases, modern technology dictates both the form and the function of a design – in other cases they inform it. Workmanship is also required in the manifestation of design; as Professor David Pye explains in The Nature and Art of Workmanship, while design can be conveyed in words and by drawings, workmanship cannot. The use of Computer Numerical Control (a computer control method for machine tools) in many of the teams' narratives brought the topic of workmanship into the context of designing religious furnishings. Entrants were also encouraged to mind material choices and construction processes which reflect current thinking about our environmental stewardship. These became particularly significant to the design execution, aspiring specifically to the sustainability ideals of Pope Francis. The design challenge which begat a deeper question, however, was the dichotomy of applications for which the pieces were to be built.

A client's request for a furniture piece to have the same function for two very different milieux, yet still possess the same design integrity, is perhaps a commission for at least a seasoned craftsman, and at best a highly paid master designer. Furthermore, designing for several clients simultaneously warrants another level of prioritization. Pope Francis, a man simple by nature and of a self-effacing lifestyle as exhibited through his work with Buenos Aires' poor, who upon his election favored the Vatican guest house over the Papal Apartments and who preferred an ordinary pair of black shoes to the customary red papal slippers, was one of our clients; the congregation of 80,000 which would visit Washington DC for the first time, seated on a university lawn on September 23rd facing the East Portico of the National Shrine, became another client. The interior of the Basilica of the Immaculate Conception, built from 1920 to 1959 in a unique Neo-Byzantine style, was considered to be a third. The variety of student design submissions integrated the interests of all three to varying degrees, yet had one thing in common: a binding foundation of theology, technology and sustainable imperatives, well-researched and translated into a unique design concept, evidenced within the following folios.

While the theologian will read this publication seeking evidence of adherence to our Catholic Faith in design interpretation, the designer may skirt the periphery of images as a witness to the physical properties a ritual could embody. My primary goal as editor was to depict how, by either route, the depth of a design proposal has the power to translate social, dogmatic or liturgical traditions of Roman Catholicism into a variety of material forms intended to support the sacred celebration of the Holy Eucharist.

The great sacrifice of the contestants' time in each design proposal make this book unique. Already exhausted from recent all-nighters of prescribed archcitectural coursework, the large number of teams which formed and entered in the last days prior to the submission deadline was extraordinary. I perceived this dedication not solely as a means to receive a monetary prize, but also as an offering of their skills to the glory of God.

The event that began as a 'competition' to design the sanctuary for our Holy Father's visit was a definitive answer to his call, "Don't bury your talents! Bet on big ideals, those ideals that enlarge the heart, those ideals that will make your talents fruitful. Life is not given to us so that we can keep it jealously for ourselves, but is given to us so that we may donate it. Dear young people, have a great soul! Don't be afraid to dream great things!"[1]

Patricia Andrasik *AIA, IIDA, LEED BD+C, LEED O+M*

Patricia is a licensed architect in Washington DC, Assistant Professor and Head of Sustainability Outreach at the School of Architecture and Planning at The Catholic University of America where she teaches various courses and studios which integrate ecological design with building performance and analysis. She completed post-graduate work as a Fulbright Student Scholar at the Technical University of Slovakia, researching the building effectiveness of mass housing, earned her Master of Architecture at the University of Oklahoma, and was a visiting professor at the Lebanese American University in Beirut prior to returning to the U.S. to teach and practice.

1 *"On Christ's Second Coming." ZENIT: The World Seen From Rome, April 24, 2015. Accessed on December 28, 2015. <http://www.zenit.org/en/articles/on-christ-s-second-coming>.*

Competition Overview

The Archdiocese of Washington DC, through the Most Reverend Barry C. Knestout, and the Basilica of the National Shrine of the Immaculate Conception through Monsignor Walter R. Rossi, solicit design entries from the students of CUA for the furniture used in the Mass during Pope Francis' visit to the Basilica of the National Shrine of the Immaculate Conception at The Catholic University of America in Washington, DC on September 23, 2015. At this Mass, our Holy Father will canonize Blessed Junípero Serra, a Franciscan missionary.

Central focus: *The entire design should be visually, artistically and architecturally consistent. The central focus will be on the three furnishing elements of the chair, ambo and altar, which will need to be seen from nearly all sides. Designers should take into consideration the need to transport, assemble and dismantle design elements in a short period of time; i.e. within a period of one day. However, the furniture should be constructed of sound, substantial materials and express dignity and stability. The size of furnishings should be such that they can be easily visible, but not too large in proportion to the Holy Father and concelebrants, and meet the size requirements (page 2). Other design features might include sacred images which could be integrated into the furniture. Most importantly, the Shrine's current altar will be replaced with the altar selected from this competition as a permanent fixture after the Pope's visit; the design should be a timeless piece, compatible with the current Shrine interior.*

Noble Simplicity: *The design should take into consideration that the event is not just a public event but also a sacred liturgy; it should assist everyone to experience a spirit of prayer and thanksgiving. At the same time, there should be energy to the design which will reflect the theme of 'Humility, Mercy, Charity', and reverence with simplicity. In the words of Pope Francis, "This is how the Lord acts: He does things simply. He speaks silently to you, to the heart. Let us remember in our lives the many times we have felt these things: the humility of God is His style; the simplicity of God is His style. And even in the liturgical celebration, in the sacraments, what is beautiful is that which manifests the humility of God, and not the worldly spectacle. It would do us good to journey through our life and to consider the many times the Lord has visited us with His grace, and always with this humble style, the style He calls us, too, to have: humility."*

Considerations: *Your design should be prepared to address a few key design decisions made to support the role of architecture for the Church in 2015, particularly as our Holy Father has designated this as the 'Year of Consecrated Life'. These may include material choices and construction processes which reflect current thinking about our environmental stewardship, also echoed by our Holy Father. It is important to consider ideas about how beauty is represented in your proposal, and how your design represents ritual and cultures in object making, space making and place making while considering the significance of the Byzantine National Shrine as the reredos and critical background of your design.*

Congregation: *The Papal Mass will be held in front of 80,000 persons on the lawn of CUA in front of the East Portico of the National Shrine. A third party contractor will be responsible for designing and constructing the main platform where the furniture will reside. This platform will span from the existing portico to the end of the landscaping, directly outside of the main Shrine entry which faces the campus.*

Collaboration:

It is encouraged that the students of Architecture and Planning collaborate with other students in our school, and are welcomed to engage other CUA schools, such as Theology and Religious Studies and Philosophy, in forming design teams to produce competition entries. The design team should consist of a minimum of two and a maximum of five students. INDIVIDUAL ENTRIES WILL NOT BE ACCEPTED.

Awards: All awardees will be published, and their contributions shall be recognized by the school. Prizes shall be awarded to the team, not individual members:

First Prize Winner = $6,000
Second Prize Winner = $3,000
Third Prize Winner = $2,000
Honorable Mention 1 = $1,000
Honorable Mention 2 = $1,000
Best Presentation = $1,000
Most Innovative = $1,000

Schedule:
Competition Announcement – Monday, April 28, 2015
(Optional) Meeting with faculty for schematic design review – Friday, May 8, 2015 9:00 a.m. -1:00 p.m.
Submission Deadline – Wednesday, May 13, 2015 11:59 pm
Jury – Friday, May 15, 2015 4:00-5:00pm CHANGED TO 11:30 AM
Announcement of winners – Saturday, May 16, 2015 5:00pm
Fabrication – May 20 through August 31, 2015
Mass – September 23, 2015

Jury:
- Most Reverend Barry C. Knestout, Vicar General and Moderator of the Curia, Archdiocese of Washington
- Reverend Monsignor Walter R. Rossi, Rector, The Basilica of the National Shrine of the Immaculate Conception
- Reverend Mark D. Knestout, Pastor, St. Bartholomew Catholic Church, Bethesda, MD
- Reverend Michael D. Weston, Director of Liturgy, The Basilica of the National Shrine of the Immaculate Conception
- Cynthia Weiler, Chancellor and General Counsel of the Archdiocese of Washington

Furnishings:
- altar – 8'-0" w x 4'-4" d x 3'-4" h (To accommodate the Holy Father, four concelebrants and three deacons)
- papal chair – 24" w x 17" h x 14" d seat (Upholstered)
- ambo – 2'-0" w x 17" d x 3'-6" h
- (3) deacons' chairs
- cantor's podium

Colors:
Liturgical vestments: Off-white, Beige (for canonization)

Pope Francis' Coat of Arms:
http://www.jesuit.org/jesuits/wp-content/uploads/papal-seal-large.jpg

Accessibility:
There should be space around the furnishings to allow for the easy movement of the celebrant, concelebrants, masters of ceremonies, servers, lectors and cantors.

Shrine Plan:

http://www.nationalshrine.com/site/c.osJRKVPBJnH/b.4953557/k.7180/Upper_Church_Floor_Plan.htm

The designer should be aware of and take into consideration the immediate context of the East Portico of the National Shrine, as this will be the backdrop of the sanctuary for which you will be designing furniture. The Pope's chair will sit in the center of the Portico.

Budget:

Be resourceful and conscious of the environment in design and fabrication decisions and processes.

Fabrication/Construction:

Construction of pieces will commence after award jury with local fabricators at their facilities. Student winners may have an opportunity of overseeing the fabrication process of their designs.

Deliverables:

- Plans and elevations of each furniture piece 1/2" scale minimum.
- 3D representation of each piece via digital models.
- 3D physical model of at least one representative piece of the set of the furniture.
- 3D representation or elevation of entire sanctuary with all furniture pieces in place and Shrine in background.
- Indication of all materials
- Description of construction process
- Design concept paragraph
- Prepare one 24"x 36" board of design graphics and text
- Sealed envelope with entrants' names must be affixed to the back of board
Submit board & model/s with envelope to Hollee Becker, Ann Cederna or Patricia Andrasik personally.
- Upload digitally to dropbox location:
https://www.dropbox.com/sh/ktrofsghkhe1zgk/AAARN6iCrmkv2vtAAZ5QXlr6a?dl=0

References:

Roman Missal (Prescribed prayers, chants and instructions for the celebration of Mass in the Roman Catholic Church) Chapter V: The Arrangement and Ornamentation of Churches for the Celebration of the Eucharist
http://www.usccb.org/prayer-and-worship/the-mass/general-instruction-of-the-roman-missal/girm-chapter-5.cfm
United States Conference of Catholic Bishops. Built of Living Stones: Art, Architecture and Worship. Washington, D.C.: United States Conference of Catholic Bishops, 2000.

ABBREVIATIONS:

B.S. Arch: Bachelor of Science in Architecture
M. Arch: Master of Architecture
MSSD: Master of Science in Sustainable Design
B.Eng: Bachelor of Engineering

PAPAL SANCTUARY

John Abowd (M. Arch) and Zack Caplette (M. Arch)

Most Innovative Winner

About the Team

John and I got to know each other after working together at //3877, an architecture firm in Georgetown, for the past two summers. After collaborating on the job, we decided to pair up for the competition.

Right from the beginning John and I knew that our primary design goal was to create a more innovative design rather than one that was traditional. For this project, I believe the most pivotal moment was applying our understanding of the new, fresh direction of the Catholic Church to parametric forms.

As a result of working together, John and I learned that, while our design strayed away from traditional Catholic architecture, experimenting with such a unique idea gave as an edge in the competition. We wanted to test the design parameters and just have fun with it!

-Zack Caplette

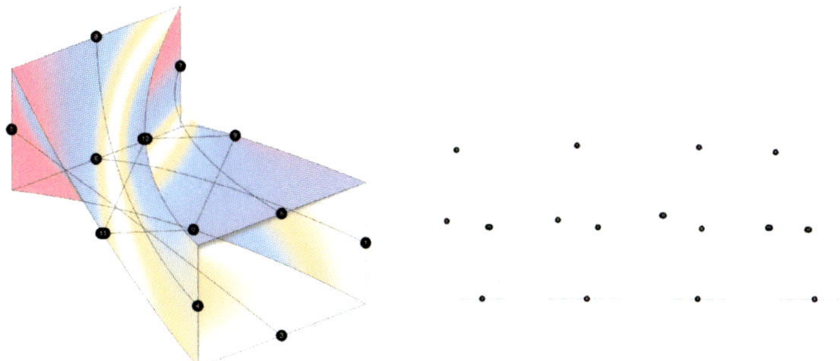

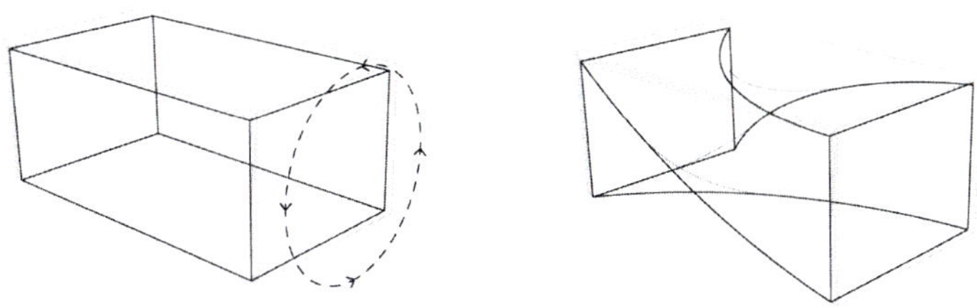

The Papal Sanctuary takes on a new look, appealing to a modern direction of the Catholic Church, while still being framed by traditional forms and recognizable shapes. A parametric pattern derived by the growth of nature itself (a Lindenmayer system) complements the shape of the objects. This formal pattern system abstracts the natural growth of plants and creates a subtle, beautiful detail. Each traditional volume of the altar, ambo and podium is modified by a simple twist. One move for each object is enough to create a new, beautiful volume.

The papal chair is the most unique piece in the set. The proposed chair requires a 3D body scan of Pope Francis. The scan, taken prior to fabrication, allows for an optimal ergonomic seat.

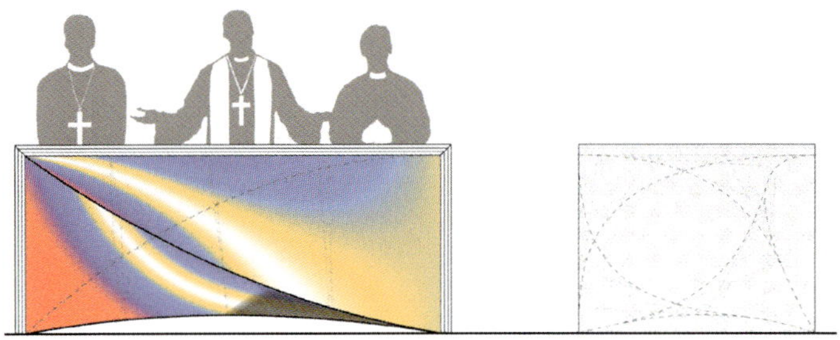

Altar Elevation/Axon

The rectangular stone frame will consist of three layered white marble slabs, each .75" thick. The visible corners will appear as a mitered connection, however the interior edge will consist of a more traditional joint with the top section overlapping and sitting on the vertical edges, adding strength. The patterns on the surfaces of the marble will be laser-etched, giving the surface of the table a slight indentation where the pattern lines exist. This fabrication process provides a unique visual quality to the pieces from different angles. The interior steel frame will be fabricated with new, high tech 3D construction documentation that can be easily pulled from the existing model. Additionally, existing robotic technology exists to perfectly replicate the curve of the frame. Small holes in the inner layer of the inside piece of marble will allow for the steel tubing to perfectly sit inside. The canvas surfaces will be printed on ultra-high quality printers and laser cut to shape based on the unrolled surface provided (a simple mathematical command that flattens a curve for fabrication and allows it to replicate the intended form exactly when 'bent' back to shape).

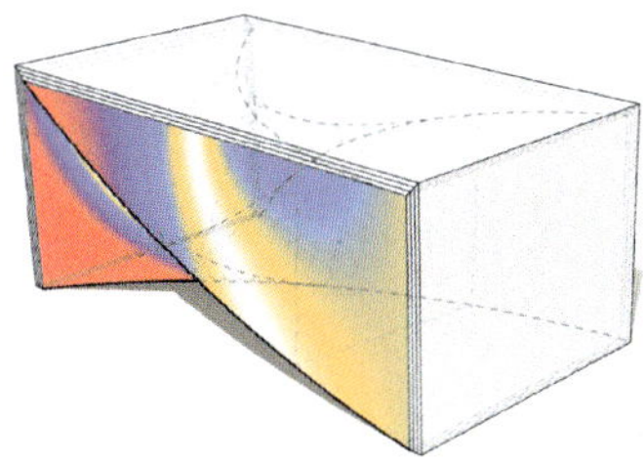

Three basic materials make up the altar, ambo and cantor's podium. The visible, flat surfaces of the objects are made up of layered .75" white marble with low, light grey veining. The simple, curved forms derived from the pieces are framed with basic steel tubing, invisible to the naked eye. These frames are then covered by stretched canvas. For the Papal Mass, the heavy-duty, stretched canvas will have a parametric gradient derived from the curvature of the surface itself. The colors of the gradient are derived from a combination of the papal seal, Catholic University Red and off-white beige for canonization. The added benefit to this design is the integration and adaptability of the colored forms. All items have a template for each face, allowing for unlimited fabrication of colors and images to coordinate easily with all liturgical events, seasons and holidays. The original intention for the chairs was to be composed of the highest grade marine plywood. However, understanding the necessity for a potentially longer lasting item, the pieces will be made of the same .75" white marble. All items were designed with the simplest of fabrication processes in mind. Additionally, fabrication cut files for each item have already been prepared.

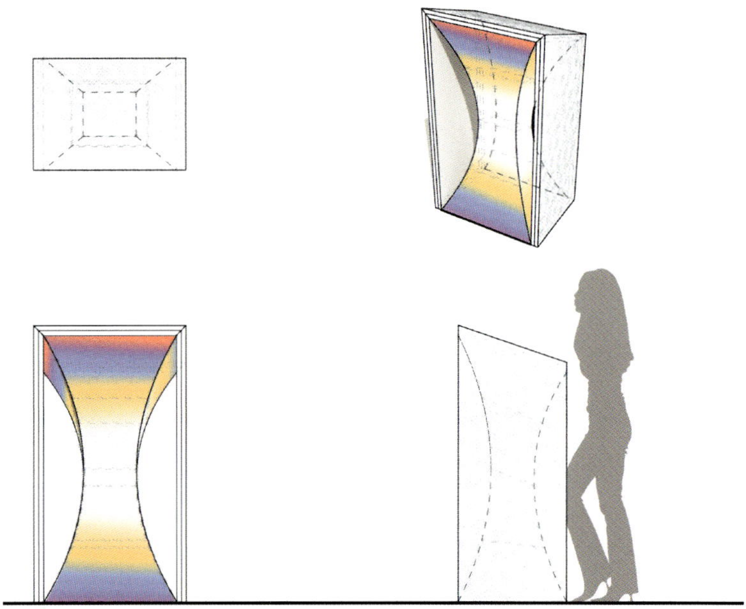

Ambo Elevation/Axon

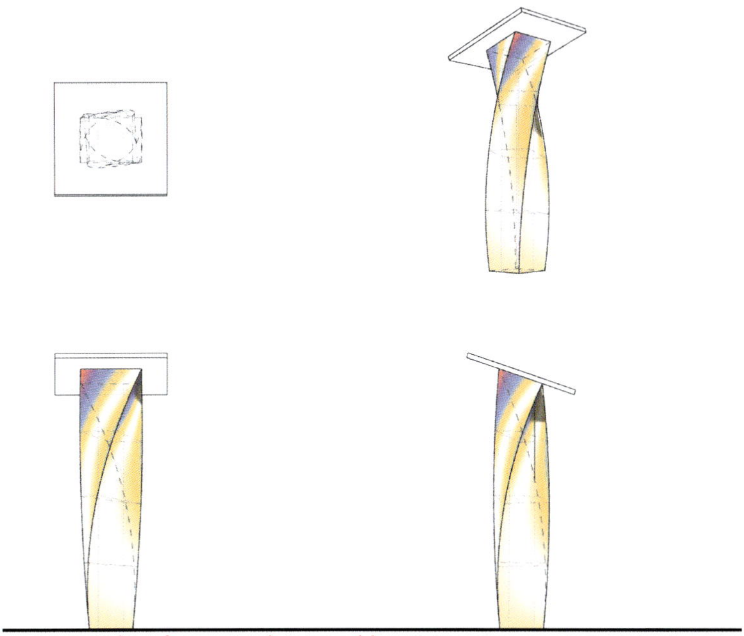

Lectern Elevation/Axon

Papal Chair and Deacon's Chair

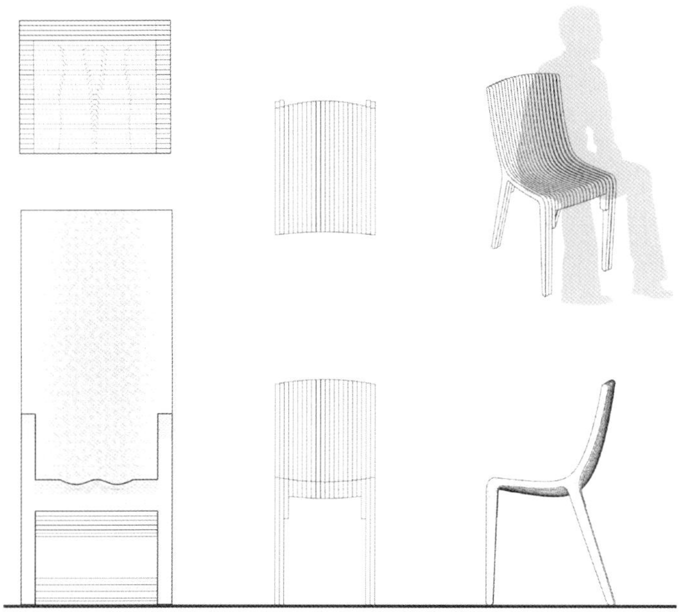

Papal Chair Elevation/Axon

The deacons' chairs will consist of layered pieces (either wood or marble) that contour the shape of the chairs in the direction of the sitting position. The chairs are derived from the famous open source "Layer Chair," a fabrication movement where a specific design is globally shared and locally fabricated. Parametric design enables many configurations for independent fabrication. After modifying the design of the chairs, the included definition provides cutting profiles, alignment holes and trim lines for making the inside of the seating more organic. The papal chair consists of the same layered fabrication; however the items contour the chair perpendicular to the sitting position. Layered material makes for a very simple fabrication process with a unique and exciting visual image. The design embodies the technologically rich advances which can support the timeless of the sacred mass; boldness in ideas embracing tradition.

FAITH IS THE SUBSTANCE
OF THINGS TO BE HOPED FOR
BUT WITHOUT FAITH IT IS
IMPOSSIBLE TO PLEASE GOD

SIMPLICITY AND SAINT FRANCIS

Rhiannon Richards (B.A. Theology and Religious Studies), Amber Summerour (B.S. Arch), Alexandra Painsil (B.S. Arch) and Teresa Hayes (B.S. Arch)

About the Team

Each of us had a unique idea in representing the Pope and realized that they were compatible. Our team consisted of three architecture majors and a theology major. Ultimately we decided to come together and represent the connection between faith and design.

Once we realized the ultimate concept, the materials, compatibility of pieces and basic design came easily. The use of Pope Francis' coat of arms provided us with the inspiration to use lightweight and inexpensive materials to represent his transparency within the papacy. The coat of arms also gave a workable color and material scheme based on the visible graphics and history.

Collectively we experienced many new things throughout the design process. None of us had never collaborated with somone outside of architecture before and had to bridge the gap between the different learning abilities and skills of each partner. In addition, we had never designed furniture before, so we had to utilize the skills we learned in studio for building design in a much different way than we were used to.

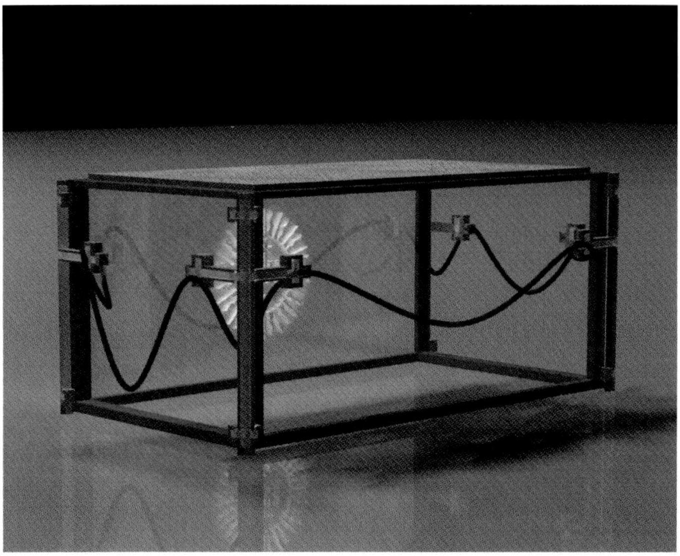

Altar

Pope Francis, by looking to St. Francis of Assisi for his papal name, immediately informed the world of his spirituality and his intentions. Saint Francis represents a life of simplicity, as well as a respect for animals and the environment for which he is the patron. Simplicity, as St. Francis lived it, is not only about living with few possessions, but also about being transparent, living in such a way that others can see God through a person. This transparency is portrayed through the use of glass, using as little solid material as possible. Rather than with extravagant materials, the main structures of each piece will be made using reclaimed wood - an homage to Saint Francis' environmental concern. Saint Francis' personal history is recalled in the scheme as his father was a silk vendor, and it represents the sort of extravagance he ultimately turned away from. Utilizing silk as the only luxurious element lining of the cushions honors Saint Francis's father just as we honor our Holy Father.

Altar Plan

Altar Elevation

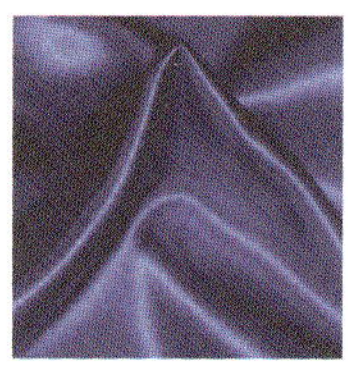

Another important factor in the design of these pieces is the creation of continuity between Pope Francis, his successors, and the Papacy itself. This design utilizes Pope Francis' chosen seal to reference these connections. The Papal keys, seen in evey papal seal and which represent the Holy Father's authority as the Vicar of Christ, make a subtle appearance in the design of the chair backs. The rope joining together the keys is also used as an ornament. The colors used in his seal are red and blue, as well as the white seen in the Basilica. The reclaimed wood used will be a light or a white color for purity as well as to match the décor within the Basilica. Blue, the color of trust, will be used as the color of the silk for the cushion upon which the Pope will sit. The design also employs the cross used by the Jesuits, Pope Francis' order, in the legs of the altar and stand for the podium. The IHS (*In Hoc Signo, In this sign*) symbol, representing Ignatian spirituality and the keeping of Christ at the center of everything, also appears in this design. The design reflects a simplicity transparent within remnants of history.

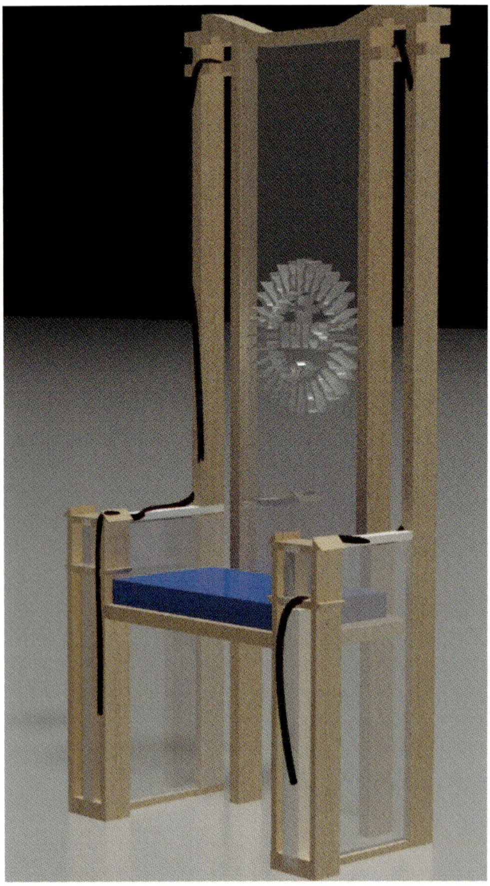

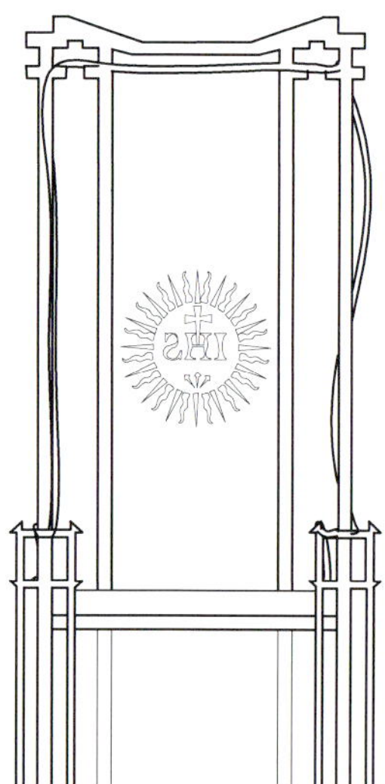

Papal Chair Elevation

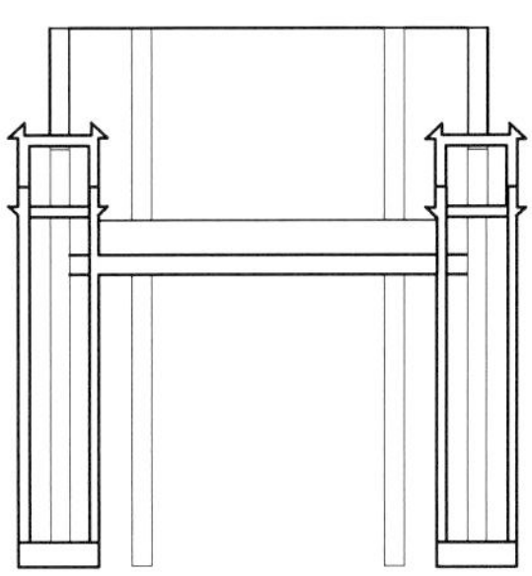

Deacon's Chair Elevation

Ambo Elevation

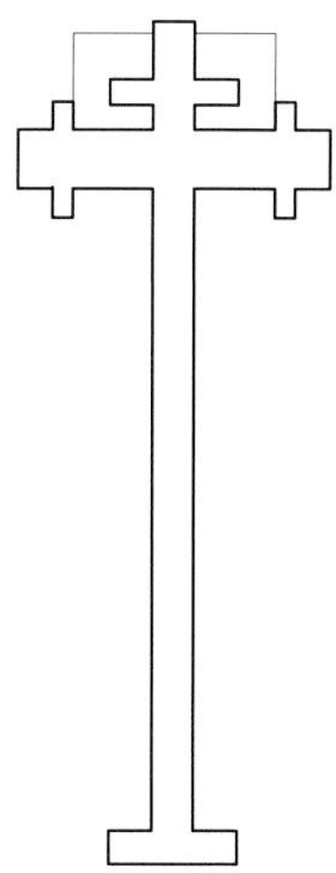

Lectern Elevation

EUCHARIST AND PASCHAL MYSTERY

Andrew Anderson (B.S. Arch) and Chas Winebrenner (B.S. Arch)

About the Team

We came together for this composition because we recognized how unique this design opportunity was. Not only were we able to fuse our very recent architectural and theological studies to put into action the university's goal of serving the Church and world through our work, but we were also able to take part in an event of such historical and spiritual significance. Though both Lutheran, we saw this project as a way to reflect how we have grown intellectually and spiritually as students of The Catholic University of America and to promote and celebrate the unity of Christians through our identity in Christ.

A pivotal moment in our working together towards this goal was deciding to use the early Church liturgical symbol of the octagon in the design. We had just finished taking a class called "Liturgy & the Christian Life" immediately before the project, which aided us in allowing our design to not only be aesthetically pleasing but also to have a rich theological background. As we recently learned, baptismal fonts in the early Church had multiple forms, but one of them was the octagon which represented the Resurrection on the eighth day of the week, the beginning of a new, resurrected life in Christ. The altar and ambo each rose from a rectangular base and transformed into an eight-sided shape, representing how it is through Christ's Resurrection that we, as God's people, have risen out of death into life. While there are other theological symbols in the design, this was likely the first and most critical.

From working together specifically on this competition, we learned about the importance of simplicity and practicality in design. We are certainly proud of our design, in part because it is unique and in part because it is fairly complex and involves much Christian symbolism. At the same time, however, we learned that sometimes simplicity creates the most fitting designs, and that design must not only symbolically adapt to its setting, but also fit its function well. For example, our design, though beautiful, would be too heavy to transport easily from the steps of the Basilica to its interior. Part of what made this experience so great is that while it was a learning experience, we were motivated further by the fact that it was a real-life project. We enjoyed this project as it challenged us to design with a sense of meaning and symbolism found in the Catholic Church.

Altar

The altar, the centerpiece of the design and of the liturgy, is meant to express both the role of the Paschal Mystery and of the Church in the Eucharist. A rectangular shape rising from the earth below represents Christ's Incarnation among men. Within this opaque glass tower is a cross that originates in yellow-tinted glass and transitions into a transparent glass. The transparent piece wraps around the entire table and from floor to base, showing the eternal significance of Christ's sacrifice. What began as a rectangle vertically transforms into an octagon, an early liturgical symbol of the Resurrection, which took place on the symbolic eighth day, the first day of a new and eternal form of existence. The Twelve Apostles on the mensa represent the unity of the Church. This vertical pilgrimage of salvation history is completed in Holy Communion, first happening on an altar top lined with gold representing Heaven. Through Holy Communion, all gathered at the Mass will partake in this eternal Paschal Mystery, making the altar both a symbol and a means of the Eucharistic celebration.

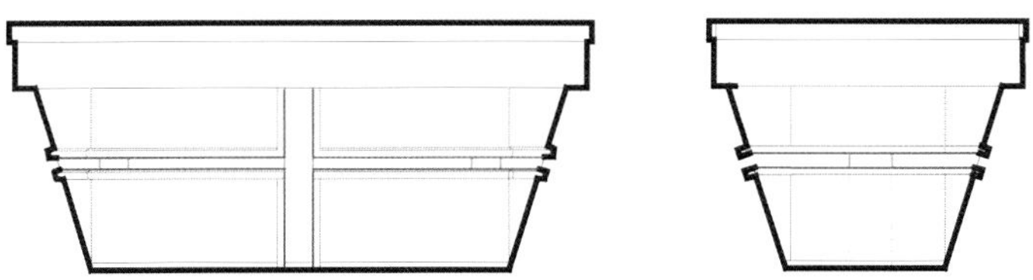

Altar Elevation

Both ambo and podium legs match the cherry armrests of the Pope's chair. The noble ivory-colored maple, with its fine texture and smooth surface, is employed to hold the Bible.

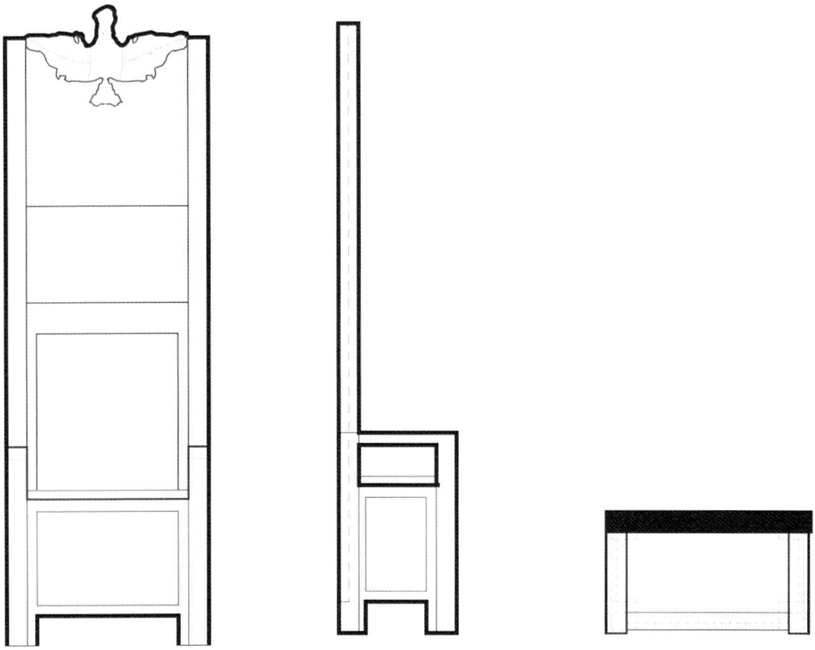

Papal Chair Elevation/Plan

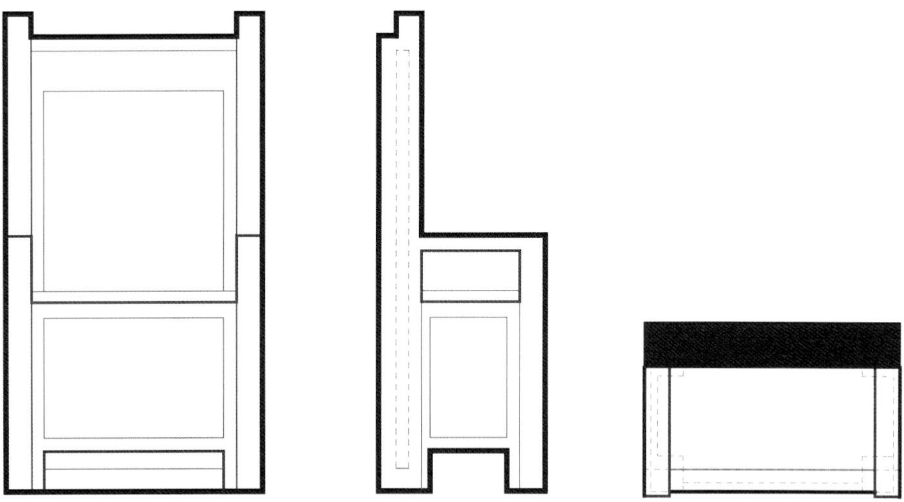

Deacon's Chair Elevation/Plan

The papal chair embraces a rendition of Bernini's Chair of St. Peter in a much more modern and simple form that corresponds with Pope Francis's message. The Holy Spirit is represented as a wooden dove, sitting at the top of a transparent glass rising from the back of the chair.

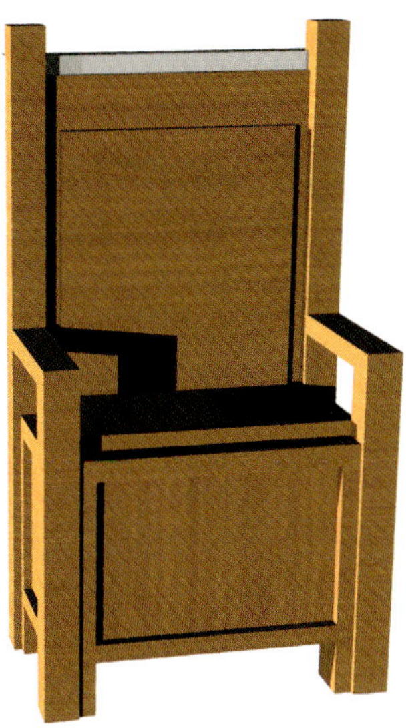

The deacons' chairs are intended to be even simpler than the papal chair in order to reduce distraction from the sacred mysteries being celebrated. However, these chairs are still meant to correspond with the Pope's chair and the other pieces of furniture through their shared use of mahogany and transparent glass.

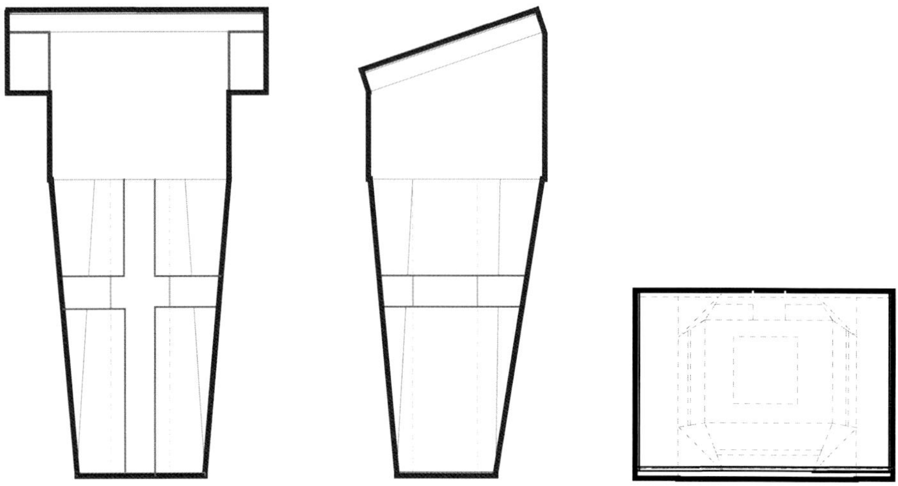

Ambo Elevation/Plan

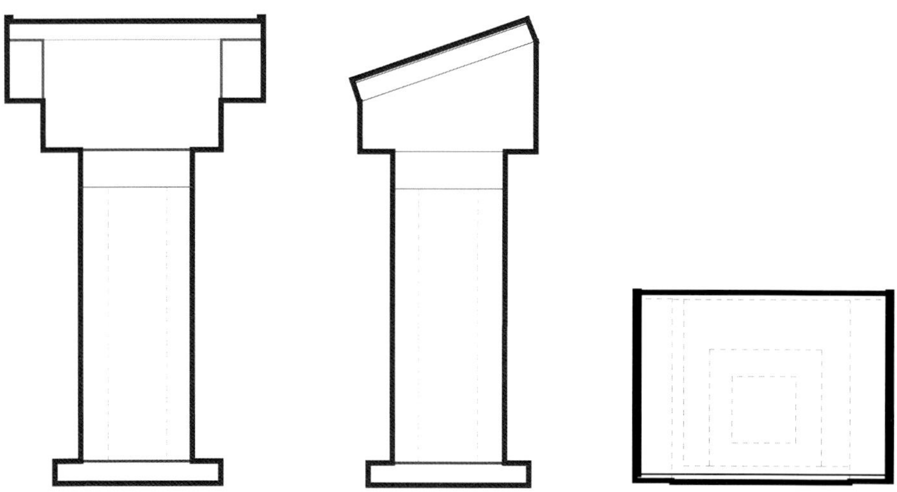

Lectern Elevation/Plan

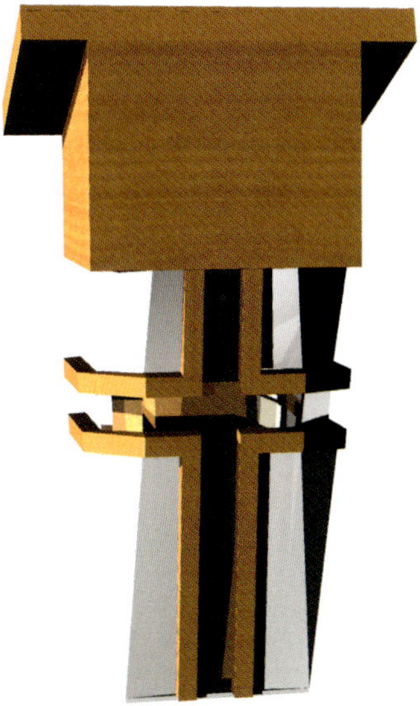

The ambo, from which the Gospel is read, employs the octagonal and cross-centered themes of the altar. The similar designs represent the unity of the Liturgy of the Word and the Liturgy of the Eucharist. Through these two parts of the liturgy, Christ is reaching out to us in His Resurrected life. The symbols of the Four Evangelists line the top of the ambo to represent those who have passed on the Gospel.

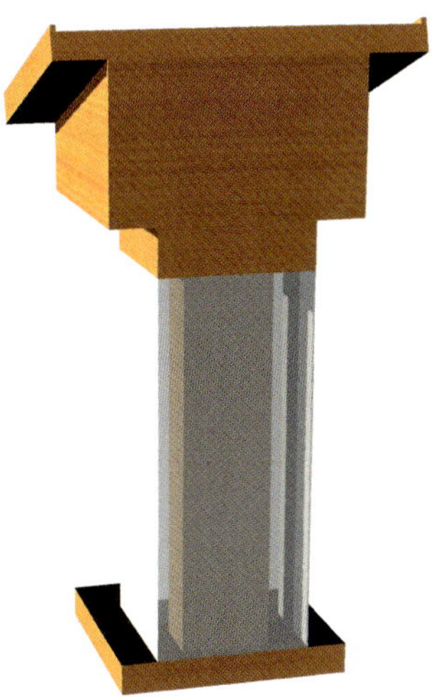

The lectern's design is meant to correspond with the ambo through its use of transparent glass rising to a mahogany top. The design must clarify that the lectern is not as important as the ambo, where the Word of God is read. Thus it does not maintain the octagonal shape or the cross of the ambo and altar. The pieces accompany and direct the focus to the Eucharistic altar, reminiscent of the Paschal Mystery.

WEDDING FEAST BETWEEN GOD AND MEN

Begoña Blasco (M. Arch + MSSD), Alejandra Rossi(B.S. Arch) and Philippe Pessotti (B.S. Arch)

Best Presentation Winner

About the Team

Since the Pope is Argentinian, our team of South American friends knew right away that we needed to come together to design something that could bring a bit of our backgrounds into a design that the Pope would appreciate. The three of us are, individually, Peruvian, Bolivian and Brazilian.

Knowing all along that we were designing for such an important figure made the process surreal. Learning about Pope Francis and his teachings of humility is when we knew exactly the direction to take. Humility and the acceptance of human imperfection was the main drive of our design.

We learned that we all had the same target, to make the most beautiful and meaningful pieces of furniture to be used by a holy and inspiring man. With the common acceptance of this notion, we were able to work effectively together using our developed sense of aesthetics from our college careers.

Altar/Papal Chair/Deacon's Chair

This design symbolizes the Wedding Feast between God and Men, which is celebrated during Holy Mass and wood and glass have been intertwined to represent this union. Wood, a gift from God that reflects its Creator, is perfect and has excellent qualities. It can transmit heat and become shelter. Glass, man's creation, also reflects its fabricator, and is imperfect and inferior to wood. It cannot produce heat and can easily break or fracture. With God's help, men can strive for perfection in an attempt to reflect Him; therefore, wood and glass are used in harmony as symbols present during Holy Mass, through which God brings Himself closer to humanity and vice versa. Through the construction process, the divine perfections will be respected and showcased in wood, and the human imperfections in glass.

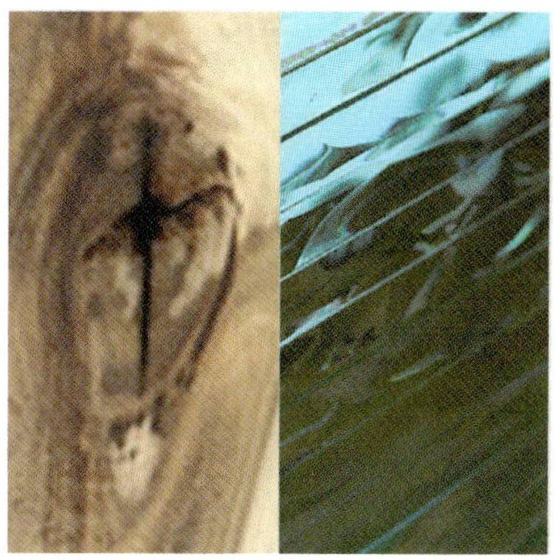

Materials were consciously chosen based upon their sustainable attributes. White oak, grown locally in Virginia under the Forest Stewardship Council's purview, has been picked to reference similarity in color and texture to the interior walls of the National Shrine. Recycled glass has been chosen as the second main material, stacked to produce a variance of colors which resemble the many gradients of colored stones applied to the color and columns in the Basilica.

Altar Elevation

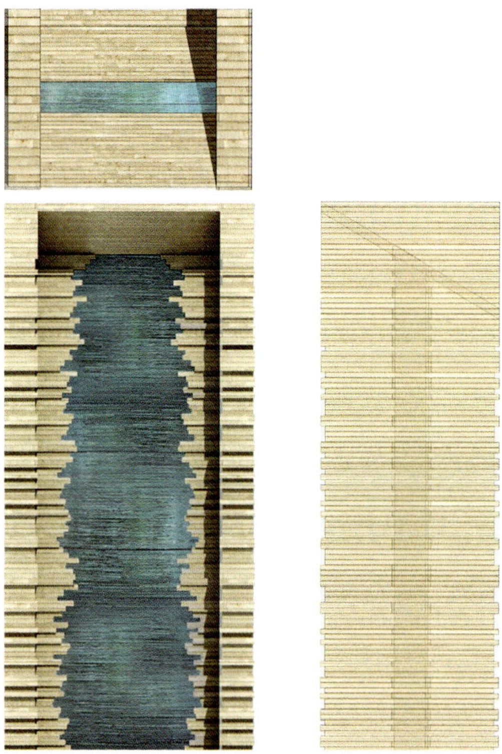

Ambo Plan/Elevation

Papal Chair Elevation

Deacon's Chair Plan/Elevation

Shaker-style furniture is not only a distinctively American style of furniture, but also designed with the guiding principles of simplicity, utility and honesty. An abstract form of Shaker-style furniture has been applied to the chairs. One of the first attempts at industrialization and manufacturing in America was glass production in Jamestown, Virginia. Taken together, both are a way to include the local and shared history in the historic, first canonization to take place in the United States. The wedding feast between God and man is reminiscent in this interplay of history, materials and culture to honor the union which occurs at the sacred mass.

BEHOLD YOUR VOCATION
HATH DONE ALL THINGS

TRUTH AND GRACE

Shawndra Herry (M. Arch. + MSSD) and Benjamin Heung (M. Arch. + MSSD)

About the Team

The entire process was a learning experience. It was our first time designing furniture and our first time entering a design competition together. We came together as a group because we had worked well together on previous studio projects. We both had similar ideas in terms of what sort of furniture we wanted to create; a modern timeless piece that was simple and represented the Pope's beliefs was desired. We wished the design to represent the natural elements already used in the Shrine. Thus, we decided to go with two different types of wood that slipped into one another, walnut as the darker and oak as the lighter. These two species of wood represent truth and grace and humility. The design broadened our horizons, provided experience in craft and allowed us to participate in the exciting event of Pope Francis' first visit to the United States.

There was no one pivotal moment, but what was really helpful was having different faculty members available to talk to about materials, connections and manufacturing and overall reading and concepts behind the design. From the opening of the competition until the end, it was constant work, but we had lots of fun and came out happy and very proud of the final design. We were both enlightened after seeing the projects of the other teams and all the different ideas and possibilities that were developed.

The biggest challenges for us were inexperience in furniture design as well as taking into consideration the religious figure who we were designing for. The design tried to embody what Pope Francis stands for as well as the message of humility and simplicity that he preaches. Creating a blend between this and pieces of furniture that would look aesthetically pleasing in the Shrine was a very delicate balance.

Altar Interior Perspective

"The Word became flesh and made his dwelling among us. We have seen his glory, the glory of the one and only Son, who came from the Father, full of grace and truth." (Gospel of St. John 1:14)

A divine duality is signified in the simplicity and clarity of two elements in this design. The visually heavier element of black walnut represents truth, justice, foundation, solidarity and the everlasting Word of God. The black walnut is sustainably harvested and native to the East Coast; it will complement the pews and doors of the National Shrine. The lighter red oak flows from this darker element and represents mercy, humility, grace and forgiveness.

This concept is manifested in a modern design aesthetic that is simple and humble in order to reflect the Pope's emphasis on these values. Simultaneously, it still expresses a nuanced, thoughtful visual language that is able to fit as accent pieces, along with the wood doors and pews, amidst the backdrop of the Byzantine interior style.

The concept, Truth and Grace, focuses on the duality of simplicity: characteristics of God, fully and perfectly expressed by Jesus and characteristics of working together in harmony, one flowing from the other.

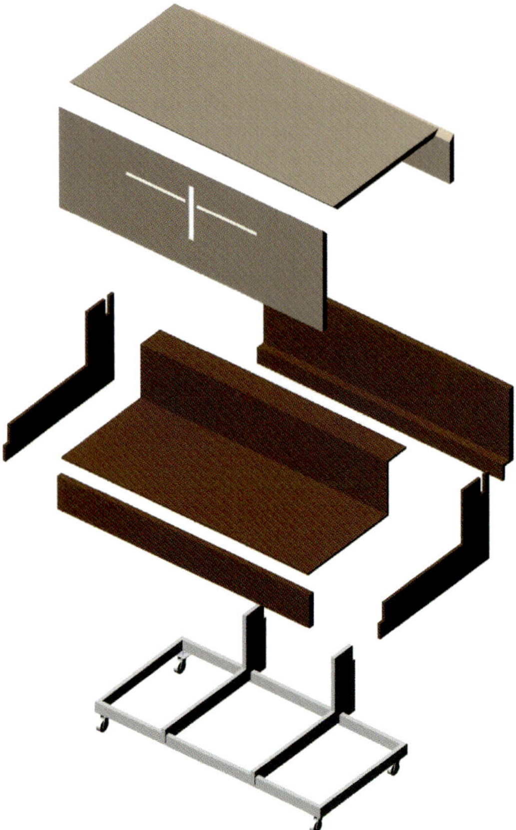

Altar Exploded Axon

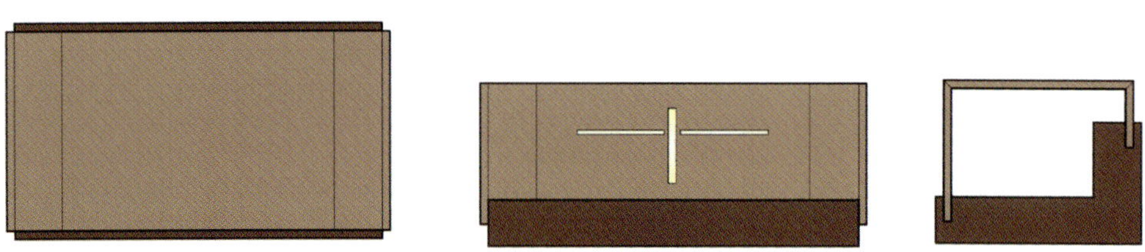

Altar Elevation

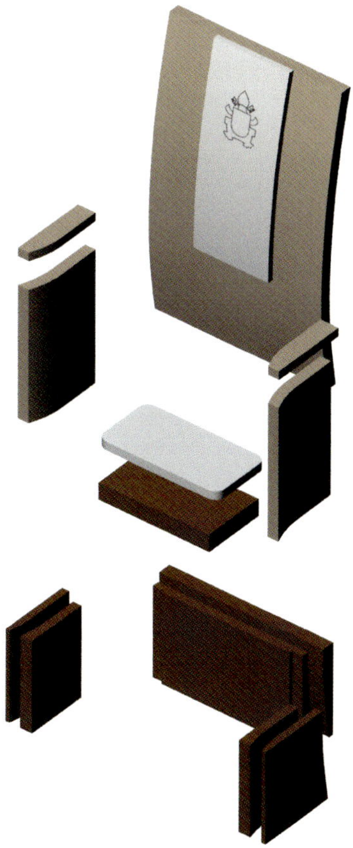

Papal Chair Exploded Axon

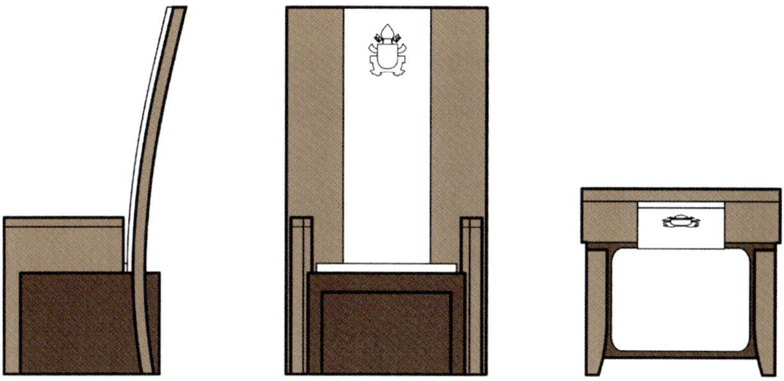

Papal Chair Elevation

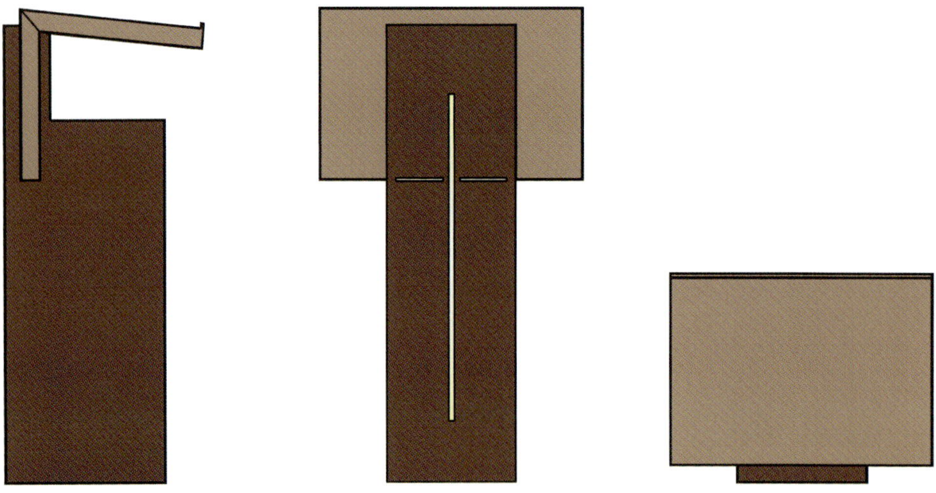

Ambo Elevation/Plan

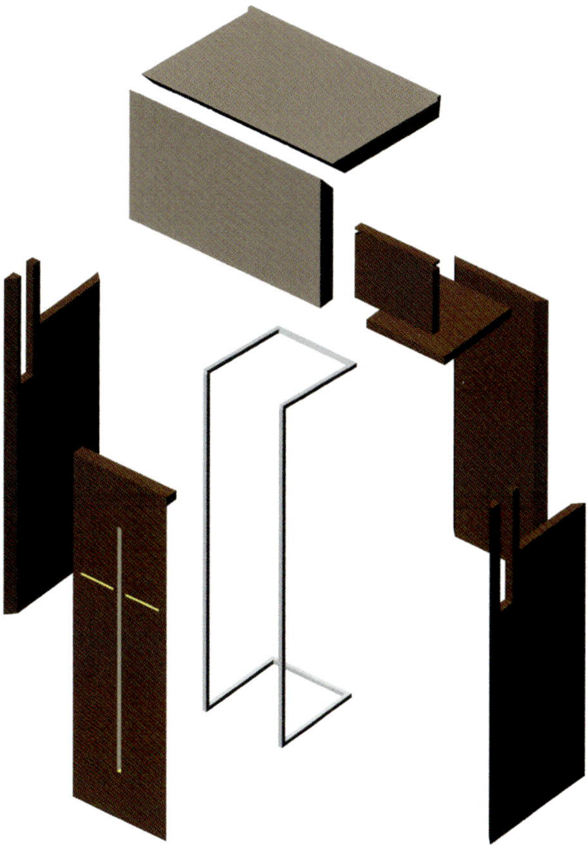

Ambo Exploded Axon

Ambo/Altar/Papal Chair Model

BEAUTY THROUGH NOBLE SIMPLICITY AND RESPONSIVE TIMELESSNESS

Joseph Taylor (B.S. Arch), Ariadne Cerritelli (M. Arch) and Matthew Hoffman (M. Arch)
1st Place Winner

About the Team

I asked Ariadne to be on my team because I knew how hard of a worker she is, the success of her projects, and her faith and friendship. Joe asked me to be on our team because he knew this was something that I would put a lot of energy into, and it was something I've been interested in for a while. We thought that since all three of us pray and work together, we would enter together.

The pivotal moment came when we were in the Shrine and came to the consensus that we were going to take a contextual approach. It was then we decided to use the columns and arches as our principal design elements.

We learned that, even under the project constraints, when you are passionate about something, great things can come forth. Time may not be on our side, but we can definitely work with it and not let it stifle us.

-Matthew Hoffman

Altar/Ambo/Lectern Perspective

This design responds to the existing condition in a dignified and simplified manner to fit the permanence of the Shrine and to suit the desires of Pope Francis' lifestyle. The arch is combined with a refined design while incorporating the same materials already utilized in the Shrine to respond to the traditional Byzantine style of the Basilica while also maintaining the element of simplicity. The strength and character of the stone gives the pieces a sense of purpose fit for the holy liturgies, while the timeless detailing is symbolic of the Faith. The papal chair is designed to bring focus not on itself but on the Vicar of Christ himself who will preach from it.

Altar Interior Perspective

TO RECEIVE POWER AND RICHES

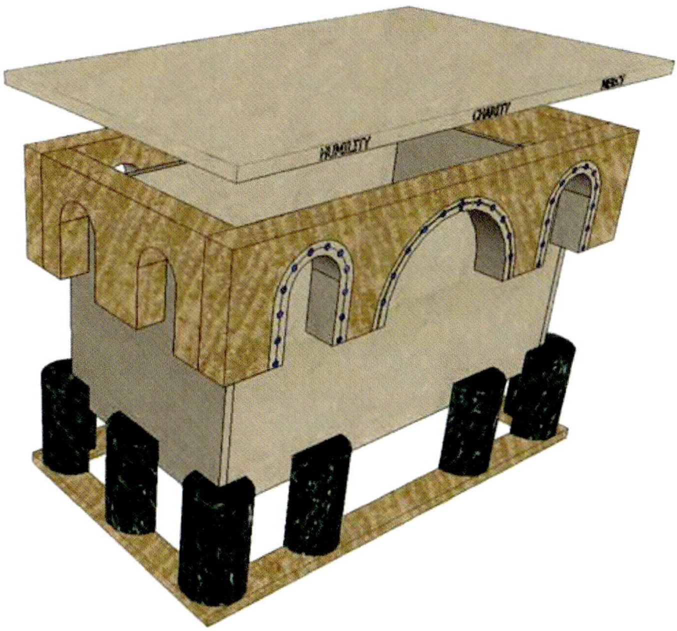

Altar Exploded Axon

The four altar columns represent the four vows that every Jesuit, including Pope Francis, takes. The three altar arches reference the Holy Trinity. The Calatrava cross (on banner) appears on the Coat of Arms of Buenos Aires (the seat of Cardinal Jorge Bergoglio's diocese) and is a symbol of Spanish knighthood, which Saint Junípero Serra would have recognized. The yellow and white banner alludes to the colors of Vatican City and the eagle on the ambo references Saint John the Evangelist. This interplay of symbols cast in timeless pieces responds to the noble simplicity of our Holy Father.

Altar Elevation

Ambo Exploded Axon

Papal Chair

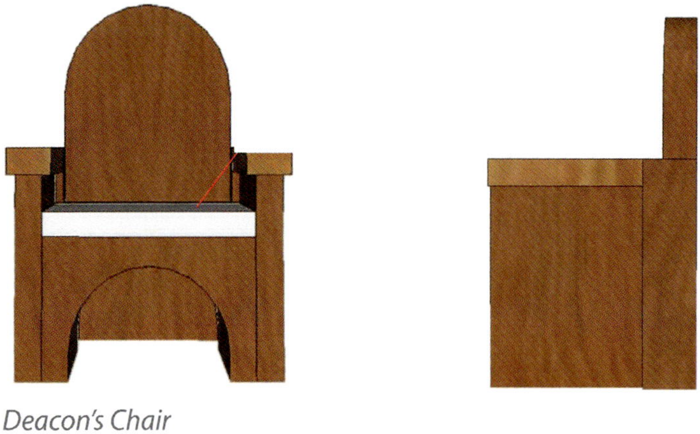

Deacon's Chair

The Papal Crest originally designed for this piece was requested to be removed.

These images show the fabrication process of the altar.

TRANSCENDING TOWARDS TRUTH

Michael Klucsik (M. Arch) and Mac Hutchinson (B.S. Arch)

About the Team

The two of us have been long time friends who share an interest in architecture but never had the chance to share a project. The papal charrette was an ideal opportunity for us to work together as we knew we shared a similar appreciation of aesthetics. However, our working styles were very different and the collaboration led to an exciting project.

We chose to use materials in their raw, honest and unaltered forms for functional and aesthetic purposes. We felt that the gesture was a decision that our undergraduate architectural education truly allowed us to make and was very gratifying for us to finally apply what we had learned.

Pope Francis is a champion of both patience and humility and it was gratifying for us to share an attitude the Pope has mastered. We learned a wealth of knowledge from the virtues of Pope Francis and expressed it via a built language.

This design expresses symbols and forms which intend to transcend ideas about seeking and finding truth. For example, the idea of a void, a sense of disconnect, a space, can be connected and fulfilled by the truth. Simultaneously, the design also symbolizes the journey towards the light, how our relationship with God can grow, and how we can come closer to the truth.

To arrive at this greater truth and to be closer to God we must first find truth within ourselves, within the people around us, and within the world, an idea inspired by Pope Francis' life and work. To reach this truth, humility, charity and mercy are reflected in the simplicity and honesty of the design. The circle symbolizes the Truth and God, and the design purposely expresses the papal chair to be lowest in order to symbolize the Pope's humbleness. It is also because he is closest to the truth that the space wherein he sits is closest to the circular form. The void within the ambo and the cantor's podium symbolize the sense of disconnect between people, the world and God. The Word that is read or sung sits over the void creating a connection, bringing its truth to the audience. The altar creates a space from which truth can grow and the symbol of truth, a circle, expresses the movement towards truth and the transcendence of void to the truth that God gives to humanity.

Ambo Elevation

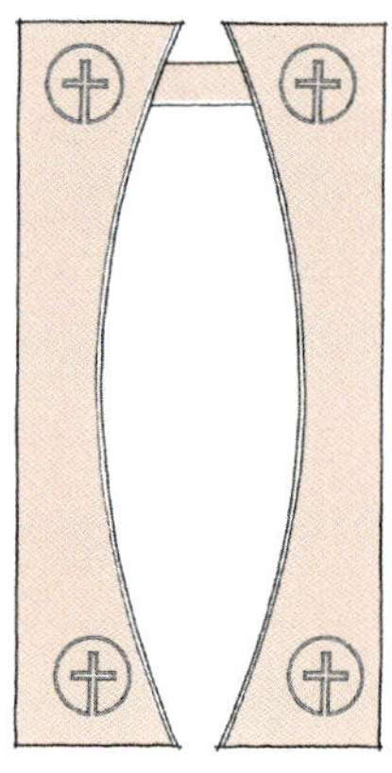

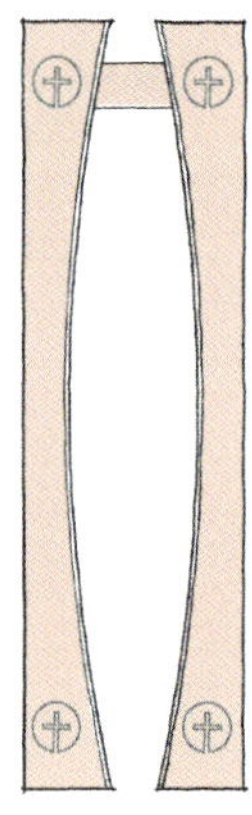

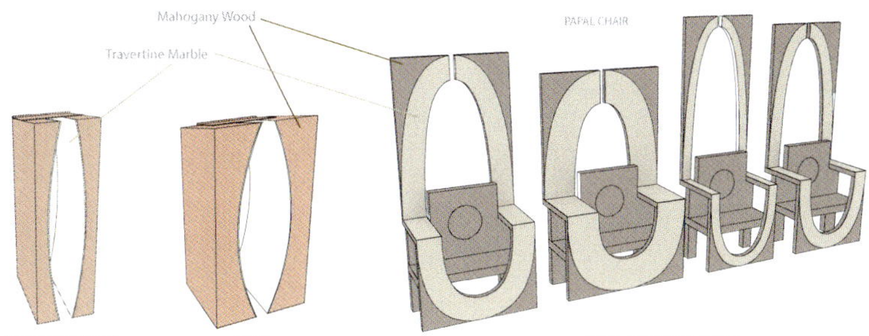

All of the furniture in this design will be assembled via the interlocking and fastening of components in order to keep the furniture as pure as the celebration of the mass. To ensure this, no foreign substances such as adhesives or screws will be employed. Doing so articulates truth and honesty in materials, in construction and through historical references. The Basilica was constructed in a similar fashion, made entirely of stone, brick, tile and mortar, and without the use of steel structural beams, framing work or columns. This assembly of papal furniture is a multi-dimensional reflection of a new concept within a timeless landmark.

Deacon's Chair/ Papal Chair Elevation

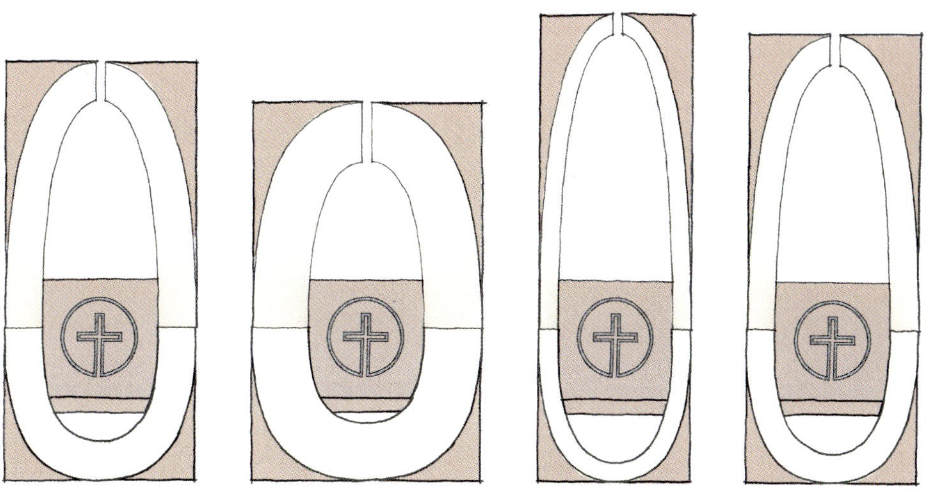

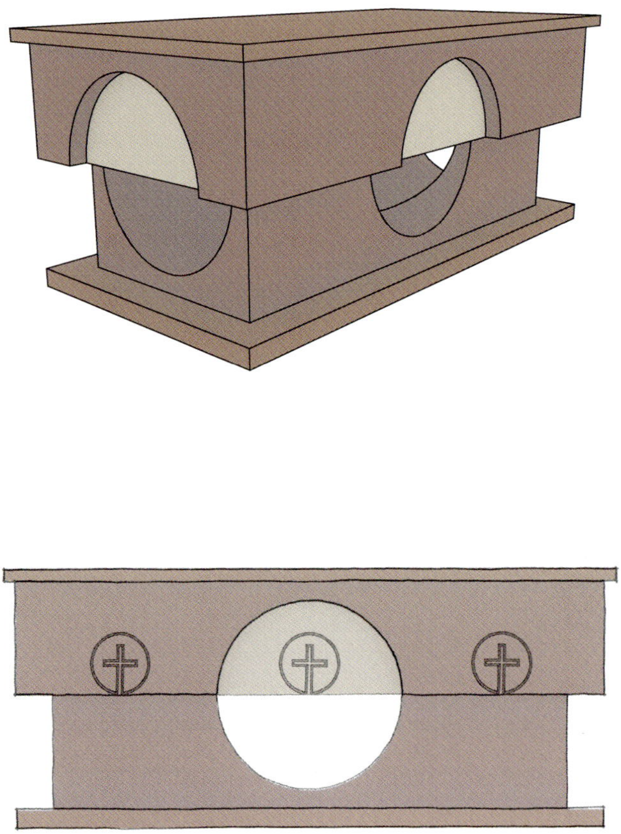

Altar Axon/Elevation

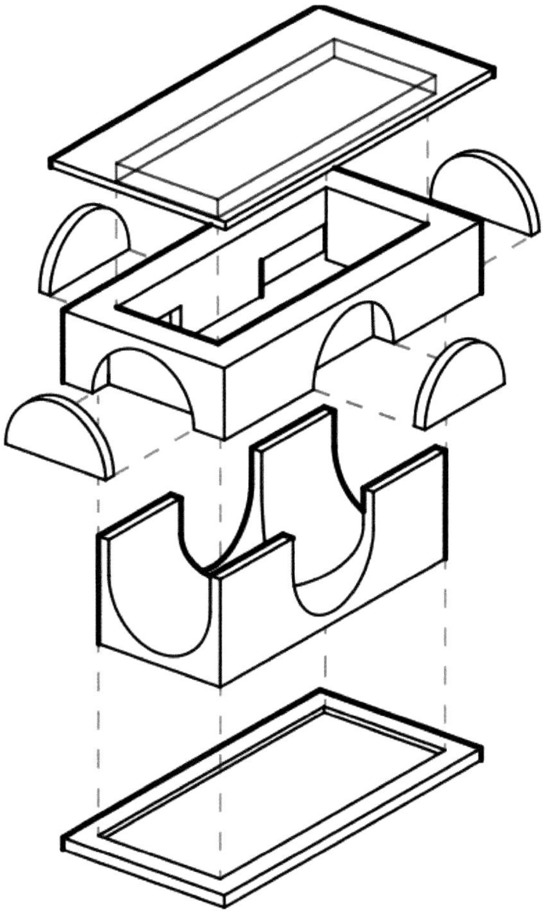

Altar Exploded Axon

The materials for the furniture were selected based purely on contextual relationships. The marble of the Basilica is reflected in the marble half-circle slab located on each of the altar's four sides, as well as within the ambo, cantor's podium and chairs. Wood will be used in an effort to provide a direct visual relationship between the material of the congregation's pews and the presiding papal and deacons' chairs. The design establishes a relationship that still accommodates hierarchy in form and location, yet equality in the eyes of God. Ultimately, the material choice connects congregation to priest, man to structure, and the structure to God, seeking to transcend truth in form.

The Steps

Alyssa Lapan (M. Arch), Brendan Murphy (M. Arch + MSSD) and Fr. John Mellein (Ph.D. Philosophy)

3rd Place Winner

About the Team

We were introduced to each other by a professor at the Catholic University of America. After being introduced through email, we decided we would be a compatible team and would be able to work together to create a design.

Brendan and Alyssa had come up with some really excellent ideas by the time I joined the team. So, the main thrust of the project is the result of their creativity and skill. We decided to do a site visit, and the tour of the Shrine gave me the context I needed to see how the ideas would fulfill their purpose. I believe that the site visit also helped to suggest some modifications to their design.

It was really great for me (a priest) to work so closely with two architects. Their sense of reverence and respect for the project was inspiring. I was really impressed by the way they were able to apply modern techniques (CNC tools) to traditional materials (wood, stone) to create something original with a modern yet timeless feel in a cost effective way.

- Fr. John Mellein

"Let no one look down on your youthfulness, but rather in speech, conduct, love, faith and purity, show yourself an example of those who believe." (1 Letter of St. Paul to Timothy 4:12)

Among the symbols that Pope Francis incorporates into his Coat of Arms are the IHS symbol and the spikenard flower. The IHS symbol represents the Holy Father's Jesuit heritage, Jesus and devotion to the Holy Name of Jesus. The spikenard flower represents St. Joseph. In these liturgical furnishings, it was decided to incorporate these two symbols in a manner that simultaneously reflects the youthful enthusiasm and joyfulness that characterizes an authentic and effective proclamation of the Gospel. The use of these symbols will connect the furnishings with Pope Francis. However, these symbols are universally recognized by the faithful and as such they will continue to edify and inspire generations of worshippers in the Basilica of the National Shrine after the canonization.

As God called St. Joseph, a humble carpenter, to be the Foster Father of His Son, this design describes that just as wood and stone can be elevated to a sacred task, so every man and woman can be called to the elevated task of evangelization. The marble seats of the papal and diaconal chairs are repurposed marble steps from the stoops of Baltimore row homes. These stoops have long been a source of pride for the community. The marble was extracted from a quarry just north of the city, giving an otherwise humble home an extravagant feature, which residents regularly sweep, scrub and polish. In addition to being a threshold into the home, these stoops were a place of gathering for neighbors, family and friends to come together, relax, converse and to get to know each other. Neighbors watched out for one another and children viewed adults sitting on the steps as parental figures, fostering a greater sense of community. Several generations of Baltimore families have taught their children and kept a watchful eye on them from the vantage point of the marble steps. In this design, Pope Francis will sit on a Baltimore step as the Holy Father and address his gathered Catholic family. The altar top will be made from new marble, upon which nothing has ever been laid, since upon it will rest Jesus Christ himself.

Altar Perspective

"After this I looked, and behold, a great multitude that no one could number, from every nation, from all tribes and peoples and languages, standing before the throne and before the Lamb, clothed in white robes, with palm branches in their hands." (Book of Revelations 7:9)

Wood is a common building material, just as likely to be found in the pews of the Basilica as in a family's kitchen table, where a parent serves a lovingly prepared meal while a child furiously finishes homework. This organic and sustainable material will be sourced locally to support social and environmental equity and will be fabricated by CUA students with equipment available to them.

The outer screen is black walnut plywood, a common yet beautiful wood found in the Mid-Atlantic region, and will be carved by CNC router with an abstracted pattern of a spikenard plant. The carved wood of the altar and the spikenard flower represent St. Joseph, a carpenter who raised the Son of God and has since become the Patron Saint and Protector of the Catholic Church. It is fitting that St. Joseph, who supported Jesus as a young boy and whose name is now included in every Eucharistic prayer is represented symbolically in the design of the altar. The fruitfulness or fertility of flower and seed represents the energy and passion of youth through the re-imagination of a traditional symbol. So also each generation is called to proclaim anew the timeless message of God's mercy.

Deacon's Chair

Papal Chair

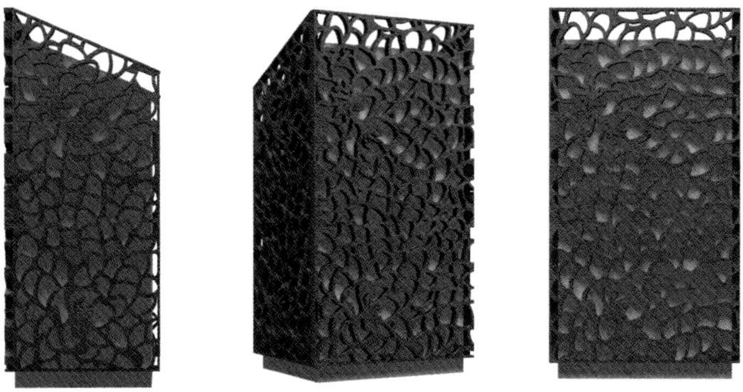

Ambo Elevation/Perspective

The embedded IHS symbol, like the spikenard flower, is taken from Pope Francis' Coat of Arms. The symbol thus reflects Pope Francis' Jesuit identity but continues to have meaning as the Shrine altar since it is a representation of Christ. The letters "IHS" (*In Hoc Signo*, *In this sign*) remind us in particular to venerate the Holy Name of Jesus, for "there is no other name under heaven given among men by which we must be saved" (Acts 4:12). We have been saved by Jesus and thus we go forth to evangelize in his name. This evangelizing mission is one that must always be characterized by youthful joy and vigor.

The inner panels and structure of the furniture are made of locally harvested silver maple, a lighter hardwood indigenous to the area. When incorporated into the altar, the lighter hue of maple shines from within the darker lattice screen to characterize the light of virtue, often hidden, that shines forth from a soul illuminated by God's grace.

The use of local materials and the repurposing of marble stoops both remind us that Pope Francis is our Holy Father and that he is a part of our community. He speaks to us, but he also speaks for us. Furthermore, it reminds us that evangelizing has a local dimension; it is our task to evangelize within our local community. Evangelizing is especially effective when young people undertake the responsibility of evangelizing, guided and mentored by their elders in the faith. The fabric on the chairs is made from wool to represent Jesus, the Lamb of God (Gospel of St. John 1:29 and 1:36).

Ambo/Altar/Papal Chair Model

EMBRACED BY DIVINE COMPASSION

Lillian Heryak (M. Arch), Andy Tran (M. Arch), Matt Schmalzel (M. Arch) and Eric Hofmann (M. Arch + MSSD)

About the Team

The four of us had been friends throughout our time at CUA. We knew how each person on the team worked and, therefore, we knew that we could work together successfully in this competition.

It was a hectic and fast-paced competition. The critical design moment came toward the end of one of our evening meetings - close to midnight. At that moment, our concept started to make sense across the design.

Given the short time frame of the competition and that all of us were working during the day, we knew that we would need to work very quickly to put together a design that we would be happy with. These time constraints resulted in a very busy week where we emailed and texted each other ideas throughout the day. Communication was key to putting together a design we were happy with. The email thread that discussed the ideas of the design had about 55 messages (most with attachments). Of course, given the subject of the competition, we had to be comfortable with sharing our theological ideas relevant to the design. That sharing was an added layer of communication not often present in other architectural competitions.

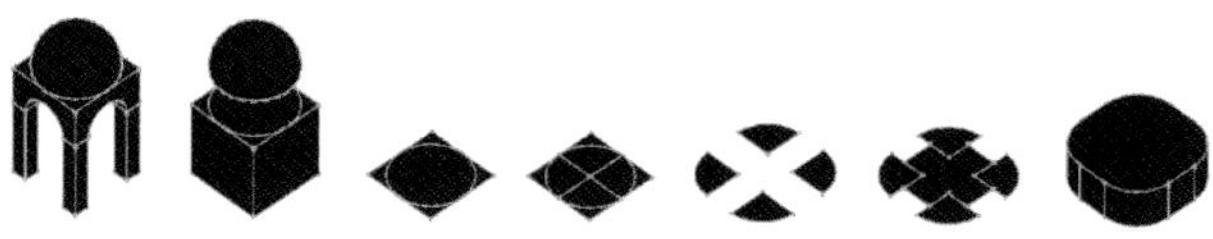

The design of the sanctuary furnishings communicates dignity, solemnity and nobility to the Eucharistic celebration. The entire ensemble reflects the compassion of God – His Incarnation and His suffering for His people. God comes to meet us in the sacraments and these pieces of sacred furniture seek to reflect that theology. The circle and square, the building blocks of the Byzantine style of the National Shrine, are the primary form generators for each piece of furniture. Material choices, though consistent with the existing church, are used in new ways to bring a sharper focus to their abilities to express theological concepts. The overall composition is simple, durable and noble, a fitting homage to both the simplicity inherent in the life and style of Pope Francis and Saint Junípero Serra, as well as to the magnificence of the National Shrine.

The Byzantine architecture of the Basilica relies on the interplay of the square and the circle, both of which have symbolic meanings. The circle represents the infinite nature of God, while the square represents the earth with its four cardinal points. The square and the circle, the infinite and the temporal, are united in the design of the furniture as a representation of the Incarnation: God has come to meet humanity in its physical form.

Altar/Ambo/Lectern/Deacon's Chair/Papal Chair

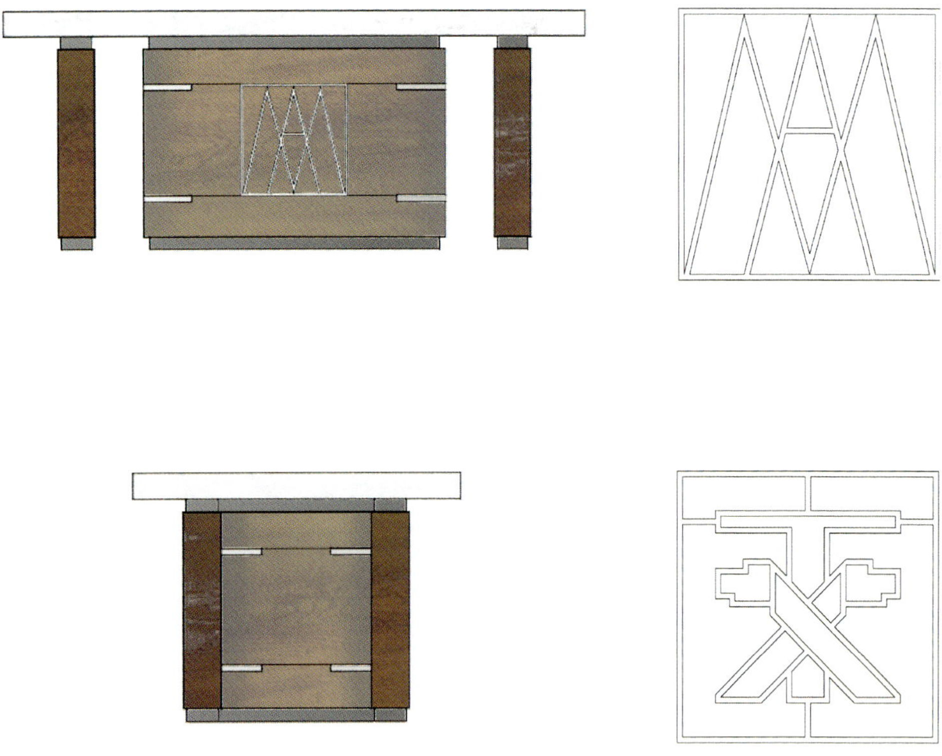

Altar Elevation

The altar, centerpiece and focal point of the liturgical action, speaks to several artistic and theological themes. Its shape is based on ancient Christian examples and on the theological conception of the altar as a place of sacrifice and of gathering. Four sturdy wooden columns surround a central wooden base. These four columns are the Four Evangelists, empowered by the Eucharist to a new purpose of glorifying the Lord by their lives. These are the disciples gathered around the table at Emmaus, recognizing the risen Lord in the breaking of the bread. These are the members of the Church, Militant, Suffering and Triumphant, united in and by the Body of Christ. The central base of the altar is softer and more finely detailed. This is Mary, the Mother of the Church and the Ark of the New Covenant. She is at the center, bearing the weight of her sufferings along with her Son, as she did at the foot of the Cross. Surmounting and unifying the altar is a single slab of marble. This noble and traditional material makes a fitting surface for the celebration of the source and summit of the Christian life. It is Christ himself, gathering and uniting the Church in the Eucharistic feast.

The altar's marble slab is supported by four columns inset from the four corners. The central column has a hollow center to allow for the placement of relics behind the stainless steel inlay. The altar will have two polished, stainless steel medallions, one for each side. The Marian monogram will face the congregation when it is premanently installed in the Basillica. During the Canonization Mass, the Franciscan emblem, representing the order of Saint Junípero Serra, will face the congregation.

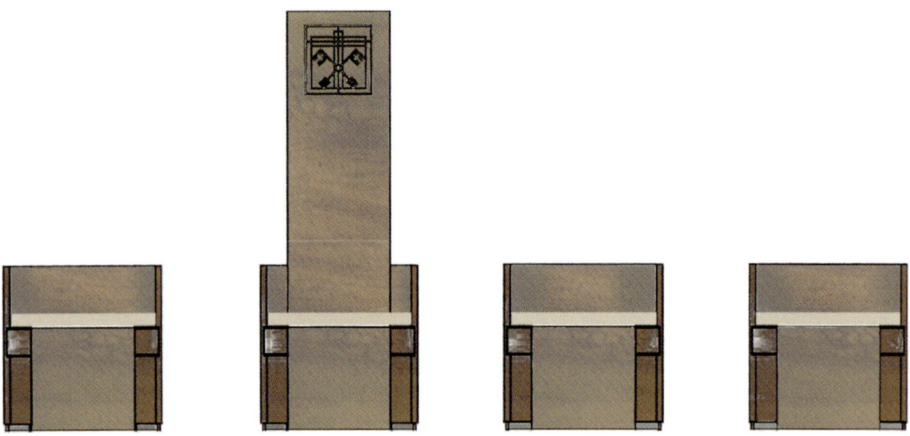

Deacon's Chair/Papal Chair

The Pope's chair incorporates both rounded and rectilinear elements to represent how the papacy intimately connects the interior life of prayer. This is exemplified by Mary with servant leadership of the joy of the Gospel to all people.

The deacons' chairs, though smaller, incorporate the same logic as the Pope's chair, as it is the deacon who will proclaim the Gospel during the mass.

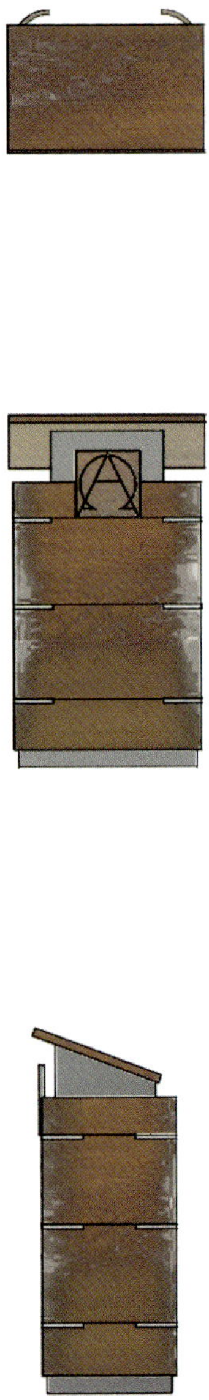

Ambo Elevation

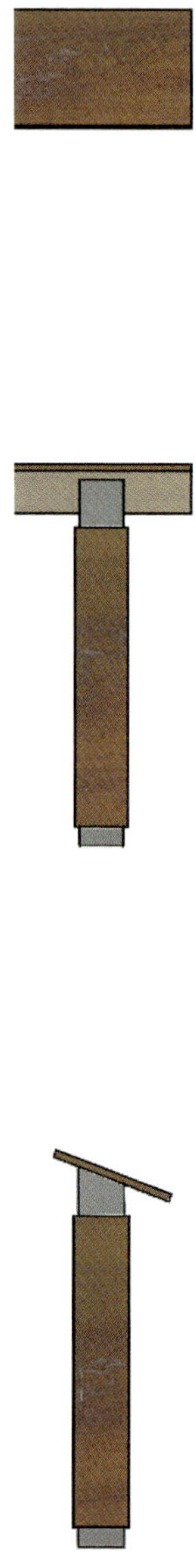

Lectern Elevation

The ambo is built in a manner similar to the base of the altar, and it also reflects a Marian theme. Mary is the Mother of the Word made flesh and, like her, we are called to ponder the Word of God in our hearts. A medallion of the Alpha and Omega will adorn the ambo because Christ is the Word of God and brings meaning to the Scripture from beginning to end.

The cantor's podium takes as its basis one of the columns of the altar and reflects another dimension of God's Word. Like the Apostles and Evangelists, we must also go out and proclaim the Good News with joy, a theme often reiterated in the teachings of Pope Francis. Embraced by divine compassion, we, as God's children, ponder the Word of God proclaimed from the ambo and respond with joy through song and praise at the cantor's podium.

NOBLE SIMPLICITY

Margherita Pongiglione (MSSD) and Phooko Phooko (M. Arch + MSSD)

Honorable Mention Winner

About the Team

I was approached by Margherita to join but was skeptical at first, because I was then in the middle of my finals and we would have had only a few days to complete the design before the deadline. But it sounded like a fun and interesting challenge. Margherita is Italian and Catholic and her excitement was infectious. She had a real sense of doing something for the Pope, and together we became really excited about the competition. Also, as friends, we wished to design something together but had not had the chance to do this before.

Once the initial design was determined, there was a flurry of creative ideas, editing and refining the design to reflect Pope Francis' personality and philosophy. Up to the very last day of the competition, we managed to work together and successfully produce all of the competition's requirements.

I am not Catholic, and though raised Christian I hardly attend church. This competition brought me closer to the teachings of Pope Francis, how they have affected and moved the world in such a short period of time. He has brought hope, humility and love and many have a newborn faith in the Church because of him. He embodies what many believe is the true meaning of Christianity.

-Phooko Phooko

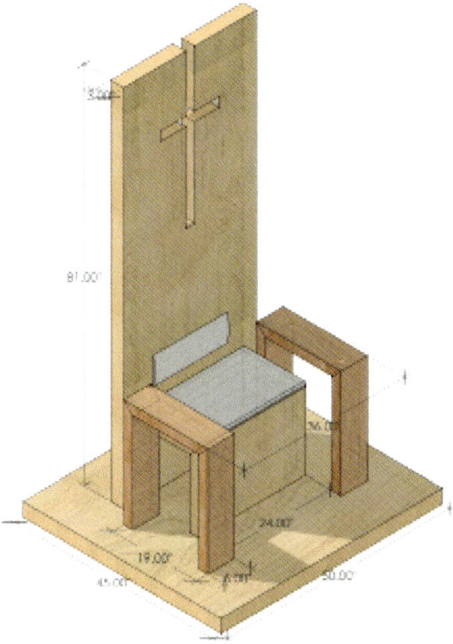

Papal Chair Axon

The idea of noble simplicity drove the entire development of the project. The design focuses on the themes of humility and simplicity through form and material. Form is an interplay between solid and void, pared down to an almost elemental quality that achieves timelessness. Each piece of furniture is minimal to reflect the spirit of humility espoused by Pope Francis. Wood is the main focus in this project, as its beauty complements the simplicity and pure forms in the design. Wood is a sustainable and humble material that can be easily manufactured and assembled and devoid of adornments and embellishments; the richness of the furniture comes from the luster of its material. White maple, creamy white in color with a fine, uniform texture, is paired with cherry wood, which is prized for its beautiful texture and rich, warm, reddish-brown hues. Both types of wood are native to the Eastern United States. The collection evokes serenity, contemplation and a monastic quality. Its simple form juxtaposes well with the richness of its backdrop, the Basilica of the National Shrine of the Immaculate Conception.

Ambo Elevation/Axon

Both ambo and podium legs match the cherry armrests of the Pope's chair. The noble ivory-colored maple, with its fine texture and smooth surface, is employed to hold the missal.

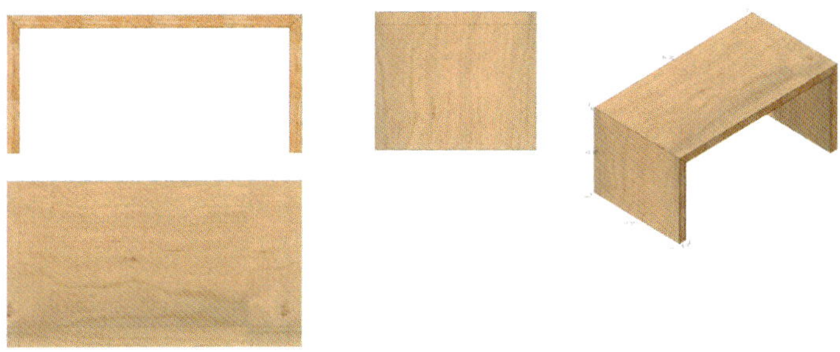

Altar Plan/Elevation/Axon

The altar, designed to be a timeless piece, features pure shapes that are timeless. The extremely durable and pink-hued cherry wood matches the pink marble of the Basilica and helps to create a conversation between the regalness of the interior and the simplicity of the furniture, much as Jesus used simple parables to encapsulate grander concepts.

Papal Chair Elevation/Axon

The grandest of these humble chairs, the Pope's chair's simplicity is contrasted by the playful character of the cherry armrests. A cross cutting through the edge is meant to let the light pass through when unoccupied.

Deacon's Chair Elevation/Axon

Acting as less complex versions of the Pope's chair, these pieces of furniture will be made entirely of maple. Again, simplicity is positioned in a noble manner, aclaiming the Basilica interior to resound its glory from the simple focus of the sanctuary.

TRINITY

Ryan Nugent (M. Arch), Juliana Holland (B.S. Arch) and John Reis (B. Eng)

About the Team

The three of us came together through a common professor who introduced us, knowing we shared an interest in taking part in the competition but could not put together a team ourselves.

From the beginning we stuck with the primary concept of the design, trying to always relate modernity in current society with the traditional beliefs of the Catholic Church. During our first meeting, many of the concepts were defined, and were eventually extended through the complete project. A pivotal moment in the design process occurred when we first began designing the altar in Mullen Library, which contains the archives of the Catholic Church in the western world. We found a lithograph in an old novel on liturgical furniture that depicted an altar set with thin columns, and decided we wanted to use this element as the altar stood out so beautifully. We also decided to use three engraved marble columns on either side of a marble base, representing the Holy Trinity, rooting the altar in the traditions of the Church. To represent Pope Francis and the modern family, we added a wooden core with curves which rises from the marble base to become the altar, supported by the columns of tradition. This piece defined the project, as each piece of furniture was designed with these same elements in order to create a cohesive whole.

The differences in knowledge and experience each of us brought were essential for the final result of the project. At first, we did not know one another, but the longer we worked together, the more we could complement each other's ideas and thoughts. The work was very rewarding in that aspect.

The project name was Trinity and this truly embodied the spirit of our team. The three of us came together as one to accomplish a single goal, and as we worked through each element, each of us using his own individual strengths to add layers of depth and meaning into the project, it felt as if everything fell into place. A key factor for the success of the project was how well we were able to connect to each other as people and to get to know one another on a level that allowed us to be truly collaborative. The main thing we connected through was music since we listen to many of the same bands, and this helped us value each other's opinion and suggest changes. Since we knew we had a singular vision, we were able to reach for the same goal.

The concept of the complete design is to capture the essence of what the furniture used in ritual action truly represents. Together, the pieces must transcend their individual importance and combine with the whole liturgical space in a way that aids in creating a sacred environment and allows everyone to experience the worship and glorification of Father, Son and Holy Spirit as fully as possible. This design illustrates Pope Francis' attempts at moving the Church forward towards the modern family. Each piece correlates the traditional beliefs and doctrines of the Catholic Church with these recent precepts to better conform the mass to the contemporary world. Each design has an intention, a message to pass, always making reference to an ecclesiastical concept, such as the Trinity or the Blessed Mother and her purity.

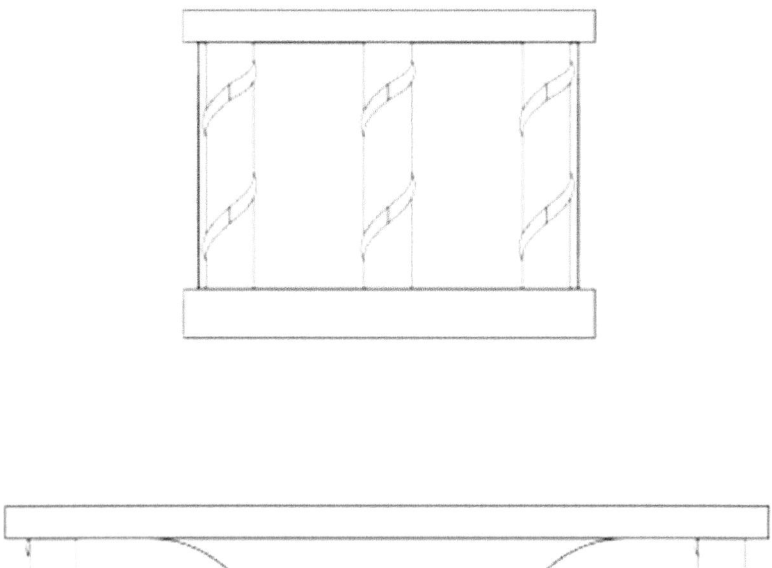

Altar Elevation

The altar is the piece in the church building where the congregation will naturally center, and is commonly referred as a ready table for the sacrifice of Christ. Its importance is incontrovertible and the design must aspire to that eminence. The altar's materials and shape attempt to bring about a sense of harmony, each single portion interacting with the whole, making one complete body.

The columns are woven in a circular pattern, which brings the idea of one solid stalk, and this stalk is engraved with vine, vinedresser and branches. This choice makes reference to the Gospel of Saint John, implying that the vine is Christ Jesus, the vinedresser is the Eternal Father and the branches are the Lord's disciples (cf. Gospel of St. John 15). These three references inspired the design to specifically have three columns on each side.

The central shape balances the traditional aspects of the design with something more modern to better portray contemporaneous approaches. In the central figure, Jesus Christ has his arms open to lilies, which are considered to be a symbol of humility, chastity, innocence and purity; they are often used to symbolize Mary. The doves in the sky suggest God's grace and peace, and represent the Holy Spirit. The assemblage of the symbols is a reference to St. Matthew 6:26-28, which says "Look at the birds in the sky; they do not sow or reap, they gather nothing into barns, yet your heavenly Father feeds them. Are you not more important than they? Can any of you by worrying add a single moment to your life-span? Why are you anxious about clothes? Learn from the way the wild flowers grow. They do not work or spin." The sentence at the base references the idea which the whole altar portrays.

Deacon's Chair Elevation

The deacons' chairs employ features similar to those presented on the papal chair, which reflects their importance during the mass, but through a simpler design. This design interacts with the papal chair and the other furniture in a harmonic way. These chairs will also host the previously mentioned Celtic Tree on the back, continuing the symbolism of growth, proliferation and continuous birth and rebirth.

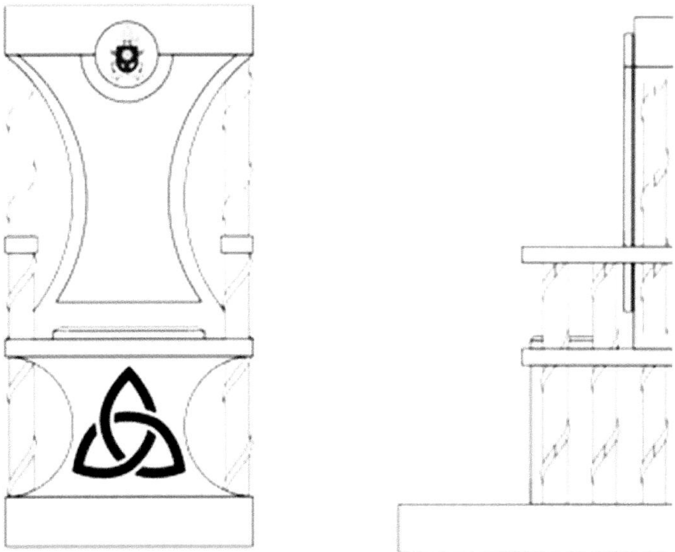

Papal Chair Elevation

The papal chair must be the symbol of the priest celebrant's duty and honor of presiding at the liturgical assembly as well as his role in guiding the prayer of the People of God. The chair is a sign of the Pope's authority and his power as the leader of the Catholic Church and it also encompasses the concept of this design by carrying the proposed noble simplicity, reflecting the theme of 'Humility, Mercy and Charity."

The overall design follows the same concepts adopted for the altar. Columns on the sides will be engraved with vine, vinedresser and branches to reference the Gospel of St. John 15; the whole shape attempts to make the traditional and the modern interact. The main chair will also feature the symbol of the Trinity on its front, which is three interlocking arcs used to represent the Father, Son and Holy Spirit. This standard is carried along through the other pieces in the project, showing three of each symbol to represent the Trinity. Pope Francis' coat of arms will be positioned above his head to show the Pope's authority and significance.

Behind the chair, the Celtic Tree is used to represent growth and proliferation, continuous birth and rebirth, and immortality. It is also a symbol of the earth's fertility, and that we as humans "are rooted in the earth of our humanity, with the sap of life flowing through us, growing tall, healthy and faithful as do trees" (Rees 1988, pp. 65-67).

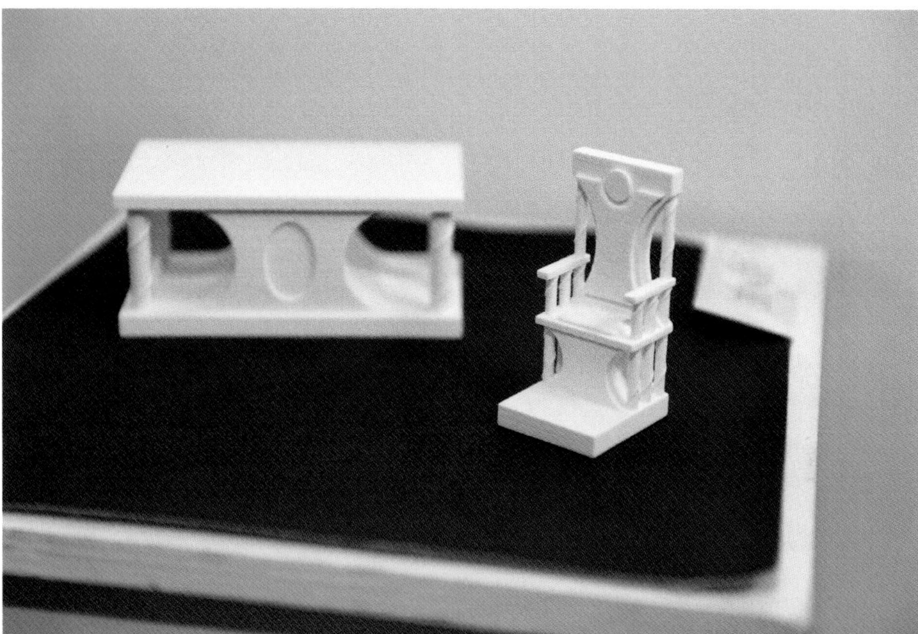

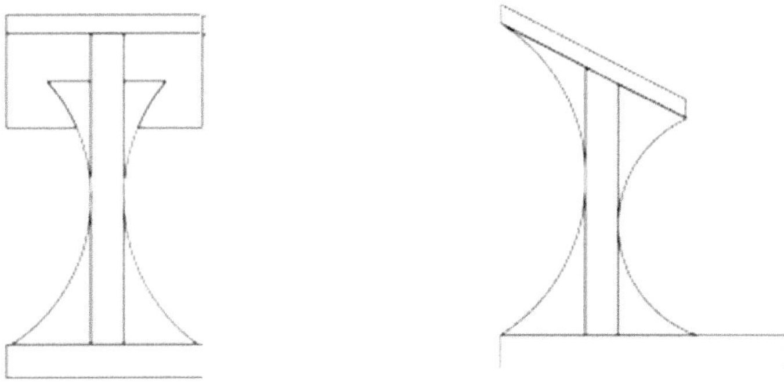

Lectern Elevation

The lectern is a piece that, presenting characteristics seen in the ambo, is simple and elegant in its shape.

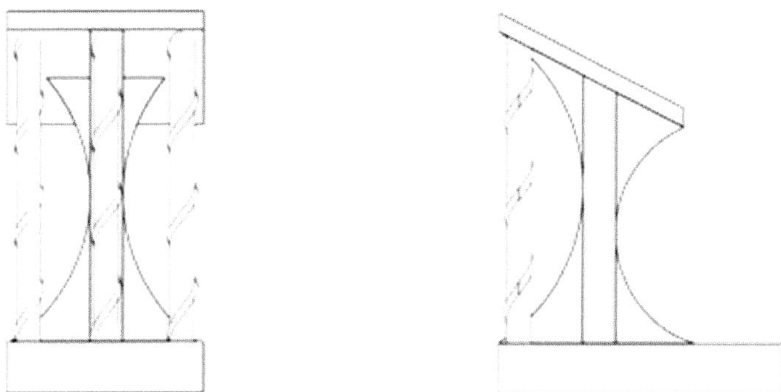

Ambo Elevation

The ambo is another central piece in the mass because it is where the Word of God is proclaimed, nourishing all of us in our Christian lives. The three columns on the front will be engraved with vine, vinedresser and branches. The ambo will also feature curved shapes that bring a more modern aspect to the design. The Trinity becomes manifest in this collection through visual references present in the form and symbolism of the design.

THE HAND OF THE PEOPLE

Joanna Ladas (M. Arch + MSSD) and Anna Rickert (M. Arch + MSSD)

About the Team

Our team, consisting of only two people, had previously and successfully worked together on a project. We also lived together in Rome during the Papal Conclave and Election of Pope Francis. We felt that with our past knowledge of each other's strengths and our connection to Rome and Pope Francis that we could successfully produce a project that embodied Pope Francis' ideals and our own, modern design aesthetic.

The pivotal moment occurred after the design charrette when we decided to fully put our ideas and personalities into the design, resulting in a more abstract, symbolic interpretation of simplicity, sustainability and humility.

Understanding the client was a huge lesson for us. We felt we took a great risk in our design decisions and hoped that the supporters of Pope Francis would see the symbolism through an abstraction of Pope Francis' ideals.

Altar Interior Perspective

"He set another parable before them, saying, 'The Kingdom of Heaven is like a grain of mustard seed, which a man took, and sowed in his field; which indeed is smaller than all seeds. But when it is grown, it is greater than the herbs, and becomes a tree, so that the birds of the air come and lodge in its branches.'" (Gospel of St. Matthew 13:31-32)

Pope Francis designated 2015 to be the year of consecrated life. This design interprets consecrated life to be a gift that starts small and individualistic but creates and supports something larger, similar to the Parable of the Mustard Seed. The interpretation of this parable, from the verses in the Gospel of Saint Matthew, represents life's humble beginnings growing and expanding into something greater and able to support life further. The design also describes the strength and support of the Faithful, symbolizing how they hold up the Church today. The altar is the epitome of the design; it begins with modest, salvaged wood and features recycled steel that branches out as a metaphor for the people reaching up and out to support life. The metal abstraction of the people's hands support the salvaged wood top, finished and deeper in hue than the base to show the material's growth and life. The chosen materials are reclaimed, supporting a mission of humility and sustainability.

The design seeks to embody the hand of a person and to represent the support and strength the hand provides through humble material selection and an aesthetic that is not trumped by the beauty of the Basilica.

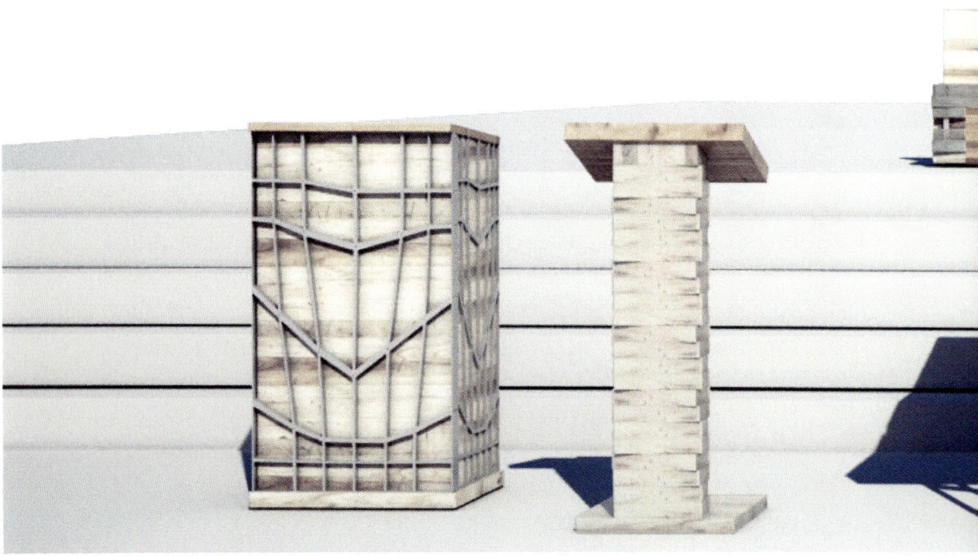

Front: Ambo/Lectern/Altar Back: Papal Chair/ Deacon's Chair

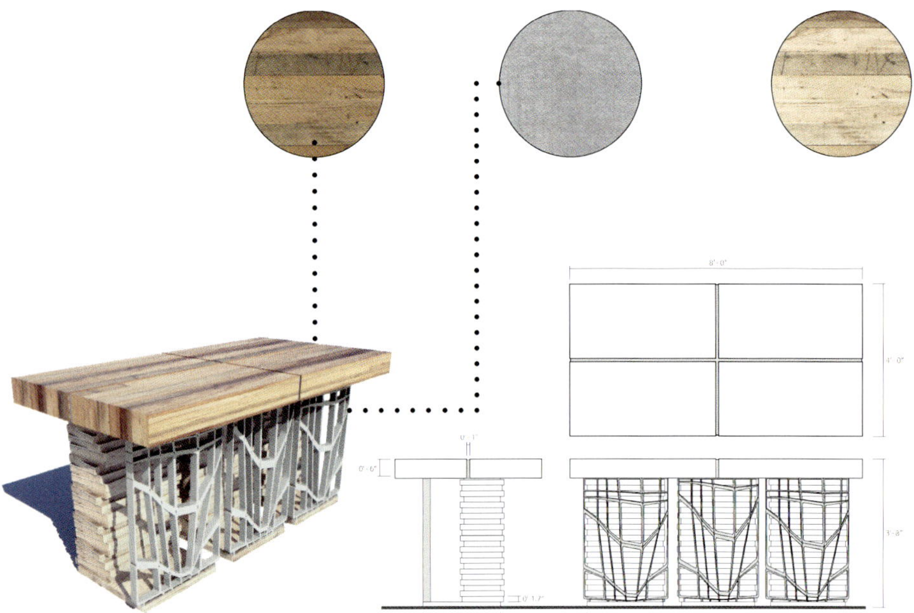

Altar

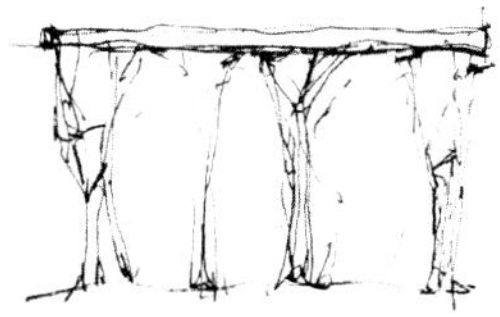

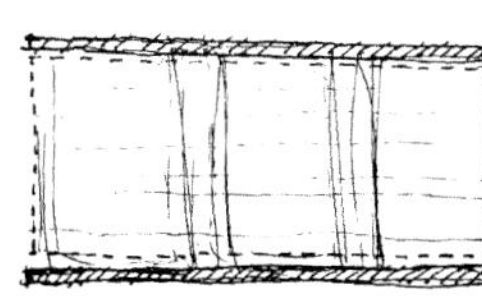

The fabrication and construction of the furniture will be accomplished simply and elegantly with the help of a CNC mill. The ornamental metal finish on the altar and ambo will come from reclaimed metal roofing sheets. The papal chair, while featuring the inverse of the ornamental metal work, will require CNC work of the finished wood chair back and includes the same pattern representing the human hand, further symbolizing the connection between the Pope and the Faithful. The remaining elements seek to use simplistic and clean fabrication techniques, with a repetitive use of stacked wood, to achieve an ornamental pillar look representing the infusion of the Holy Trinity. The design seeks a polished and clean construction with the ability to be assembled and disassembled quickly and easily, through modular parts. The primary material is reclaimed and refurbished lumber from a nearby site, potentially salvaged in two ways: a natural, rough finish or a polished, deeper finish. The darker finish is seen primarily in the altar, papal chair and ambo. The repurposed metal and the refurbished lumber will together be crafted to yield to the Basilica's interior as the hand of the Faithful, united in the Church.

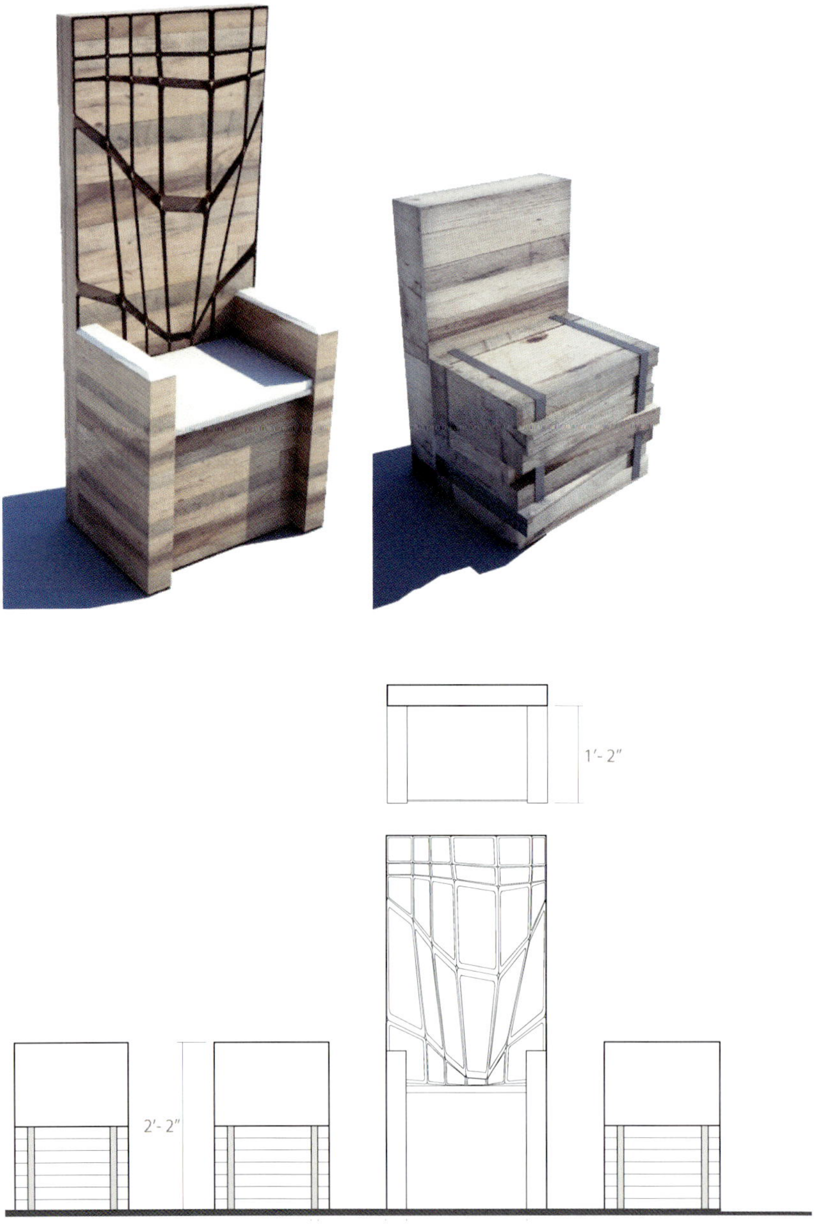

Papal Chair/Deacon's Chair

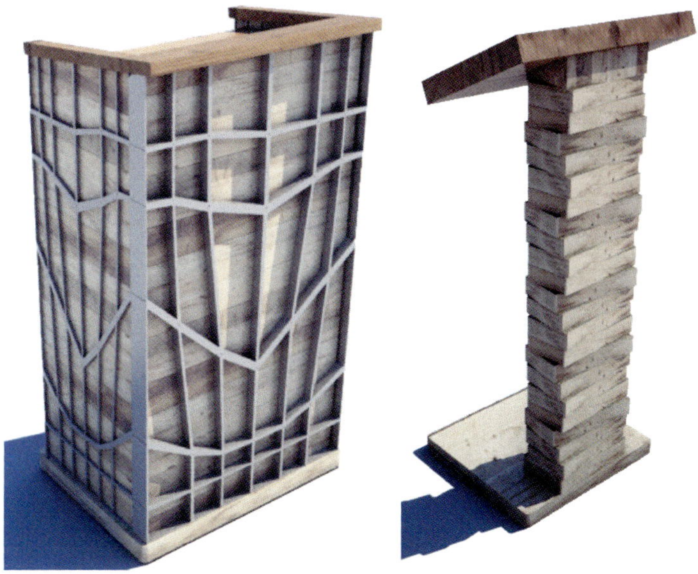

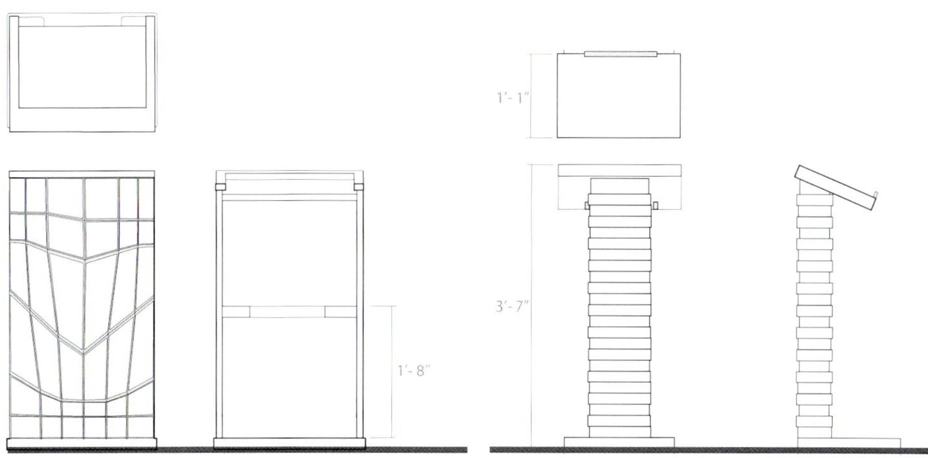

Ambo/Lectern

A Chair for Pope Francis

FOR THE HOLY FATHER AND BLESSED JUNÍPERO SERRA

Michael Spinelli (B.S. Arch) and Mike Taylor (B.S. Arch)

About the Team

Seeing that it was the end of our sophomore year, our team decided that the papal design competition was an excellent opportunity to hone our design skills by competing against, and learning from, students with varying levels of experience, presentation styles and ideals.

Due to varying circumstances our team was never actually in the same room while going through the design process. However, after countless phone calls and scrapped ideas, there was one specific moment in which each of our concepts finally meshed into what would become the final design.

The most significant lesson did not become apparent until after we had already presented. We found out the hard way that, while it is important to craft an idea that is truly your own, one must also consider those whom you are designing for. Though we did adhere to the criteria of the project, we failed to account for the questions that would be asked of us. What we had thought was a complete project still left so many questions unanswered. Though we had accounted for elements of design and the sacred nature of the mass, things such as materiality and overall practicality were questions we simply did not have answers for when the time came for scrutiny.

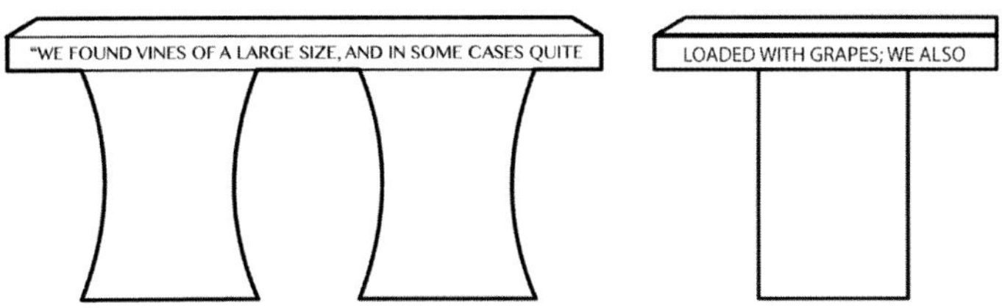

Altar Elevation

The Holy Father's furnishings, as a representation of his mission and teaching to the Catholic Church, must also aspire to the majestic interior of the Basilica. This design most simply embodies this idea.

Words and forms craft a potent statement about our faith. The pieces are unified, but do not detract from the Shrine.

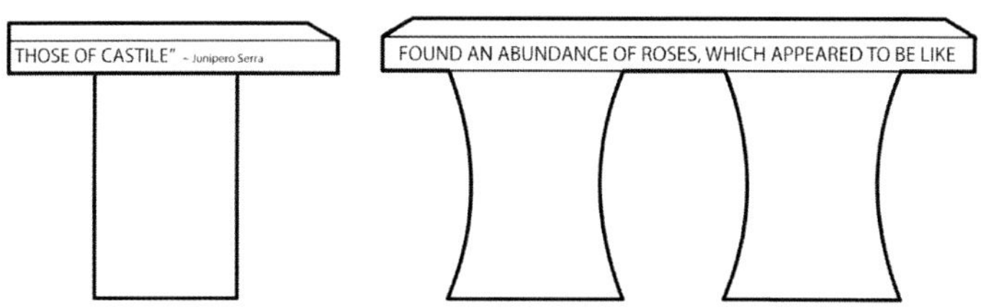

The centerpiece is a simple stone altar. Pope Francis is a simple and humble person and the stone signifies how he is the rock of the Church. Wrapped around the edge of the altar is a quote from Saint Junípero Serra. The quote incorporates roses, which are a symbol of Mary, and the incorporation ties in with the setting of the Canonization Mass, the Basilica of the National Shrine of the Immaculate Conception.

Deacon's Chair Elevation/Perspective

The deacons' chairs resemble the papal chair and are made of wood. They feature an engraving of the Meeting of Families crest and are also shorter than the papal chair. This crest will remind people why the Pope is visiting the United States.

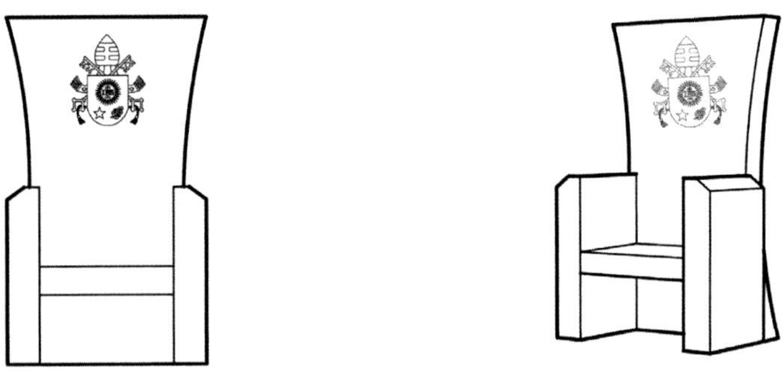

Papal Chair Elevation/Perspective

The papal chair is a simple wooden chair with Pope Francis's Coat of Arms engraved into the back. This chair is meant to be simple and humble, just like the Holy Father, yet still elegant enough for the ceremony and Basilica where the mass will be held; both are beautiful and elegant expressions of the Church.

Ambo Elevation/Perspective

The ambo is a replica of the base of the altar, and also made of stone to symbolize the Word of God which will be spoken there. It is the base of the Eucharist that is celebrated at the altar. The cross engraved into the ambo is a Franciscan cross, reflecting Saint Junípero Serra's Franciscan order, St. Francis' mission, and our Holy Father's name.

Cantor's Podium Elevation/Perspective

The cantor's podium is a complementary yet less complex version of the ambo. It features the same cross engraved into the wood as well as the same form as the base of the altar. These overarching features reference that the Word of God is often heard in music as well as being spoken. The symbolism of these pieces reflects the unity of the Canonization Mass and subsequent permanence in the Basilica in a very simple and unambiguous language. Text, material, and form unite to pay homage to the Holy Father and to Saint Junípero Serra while creating a solid base for future masses in the Basilica.

3'9" H

SANCTUARY, GEOMETRY, AND NATURE

William Sullivan (B.S. Arch) and Dennis Nilsen (Ph.D. Candidate in Politics)

Honorable Mention Winner

About the Team

Coming from diverse academic backgrounds - architecture and politics - we had only twelve days to create a scheme, design and competition brief. We had previously worked together to submit a design for the Philadelphia Sanctuary Competition and were the only team from The Catholic University of America to submit one. To begin this design, we executed the research to support liturgical symbolism and lead the design towards noble simplicity in the theme of the canonization of then-Blessed Junípero Serra. We then developed these themes and produced the design and drawings. Through this process, we were able to come up with the final design. After the competition was over, neither of us would see each other again, but we were both very gratified to have worked together in the competition.

A pivotal moment in working occurred when we reached an agreement about the use of symbolism to express both the occasion for the altar's construction - the Papal Mass for canonizing Blessed Junípero Serra - and the surroundings of the Basilica, its permanent home. Finding an appropriate congruence to address the two ends was the central jewel in the crown, which then allowed us to elaborate upon the project with so many details, just as secondary stones emphasize the primary jewel.

A significant lesson for us was how a design reveals content and concept. The essence of a design speaks in its clearest voice through material and form, not because of the force of the architect but with the architect as a revealer. The team meditation on the essence of noble simplicity was a significant instrument in the teaching of this lesson and focusing the design as if it were a gyroscope pulsating until a final balance was reached.

Also, a special thanks is due to Alba Quintanilla and Ghalya Al Dafiri who helped with communications and technical support.

"I can say that the most beautiful and natural expressions of joy which I have seen in my life were in poor people who had little to hold on to."
– Pope Francis on Simple Living

The form of the sanctuary is based on the geometries and traditions of the Basilica's architecture with a motion towards expressive simplicity. The feet of the furniture are derived from the form of the Byzantine capitols of its baldacchino. The taper to the ground serves to create a delicate interaction between the earth and the furniture itself much in the way God speaks to us through His prayer and grace. The arches on the furniture are also geometrically inspired by the arches in the baldacchino. This is the most efficient and graceful form.

"The straight line belongs to man, the curved belongs to God".
–Antoni Gaudí i Cornet (1852-1926)

The arch is a central element in all the forms of the furniture, a unifying element and a powerfully simple form, shaped like a rainbow, symbolic of God's covenant with Noah. The triangular pediment is taken from the facades of the porticos of the Basilica. This form is the purest and simplest of all angular shapes, and also symbolizes the Trinity. The flat portions at the base of the triangles are seen in the pediment of the East Portico and serve to visually stabilize the triangle. The altar mensa or base can be adjusted to allow for the insertion of a relic of Saint Serra.

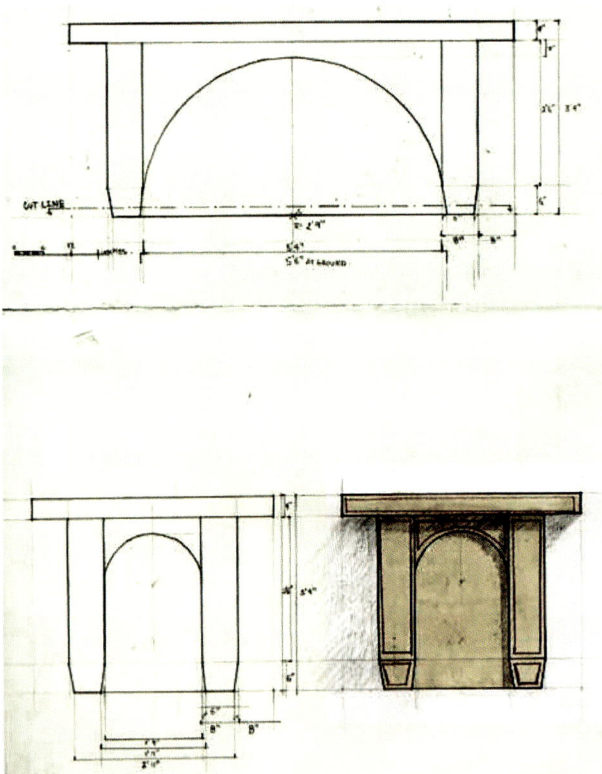

Altar Elevation

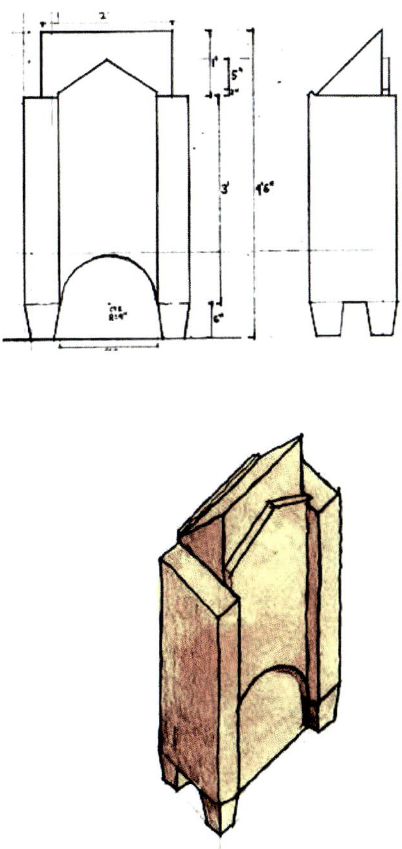

Lectern Elevation/Axon

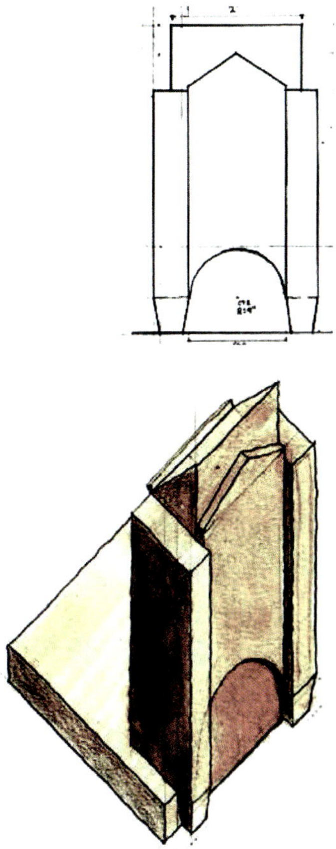

Ambo Elevation/Axon

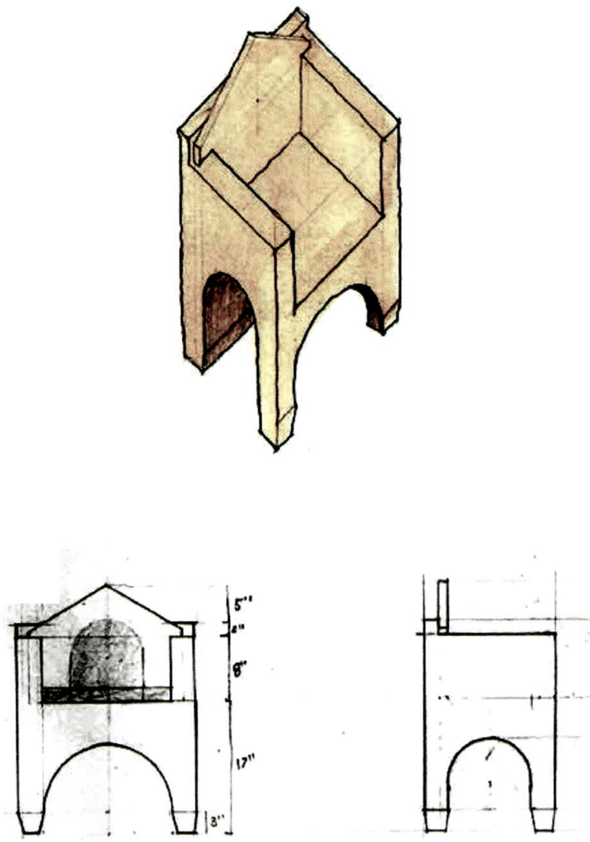

Deacon's Chair Elevation/Axon

The chosen material is blonde honey oak with dark juniper inlay. Though juniper is blonde in nature it can be stained or darkened to a deeper color; the choice of oak is for its place in American carpentry and is categorically a noble and sustainable wood used in America. The use of juniper is a bow to Saint Serra's name and his service in the USA.

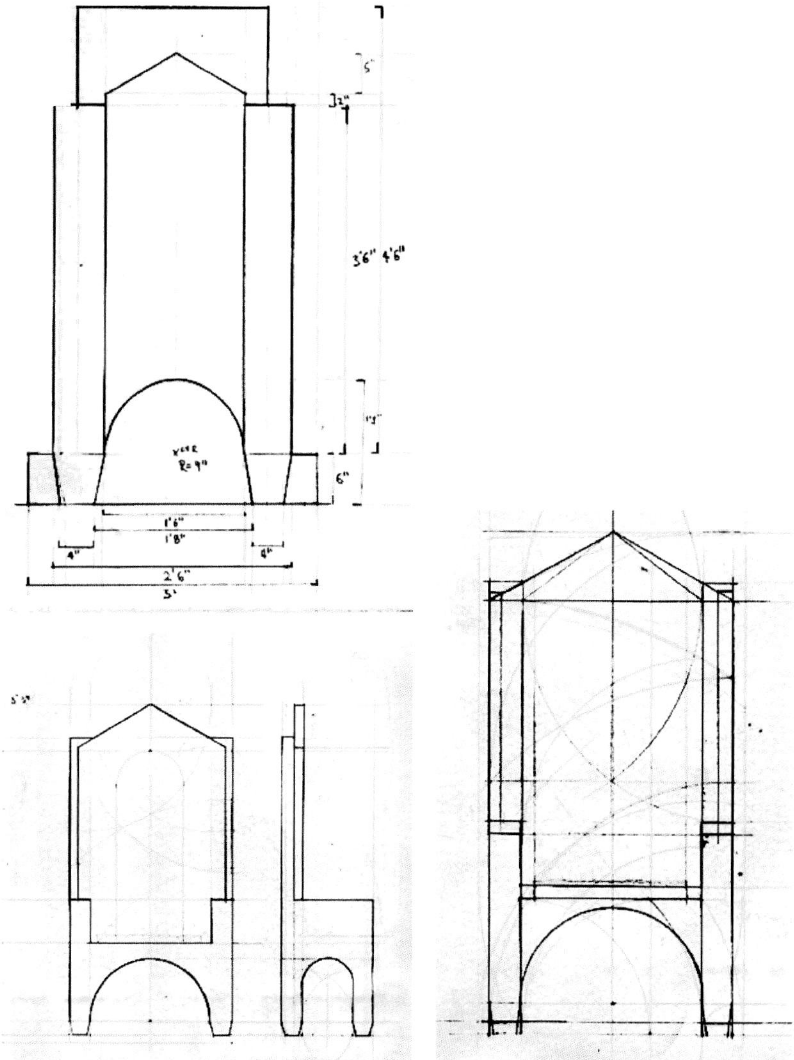

Papal Chair Elevation/Axon

Simple geometry paired with materials that are locally harvested integrate to create an assembly which harmonizes with the Basilica and with the papal simplicity imbued by our Holy Father. Classic and timeless, this design delicately embraces all intents.

A KINSHIP BETWEEN CHURCH AND NATURE

Madeline Traylor (B.S. Arch), Matthew Barton (B.S. Arch), Alix Herrera (B.S. Arch) and Kaela Diamond (B.S. Arch)

About the Team

We decided to enter the competition because we had just finished our first real design project and wanted to practice our newly-found methods on another project. We decided to work together because of how well we had collaborated in studio.

The first night of research, we collaborated to develop word associations and gesture drawings, and to brainstorm ideas. This was the favorite part of our project.

We learned how to communicate design without all being present in a meeting. Because of the accelerated design period, and the conditions the summer break brought, we had to work together over email or telephone calls. Not all firms have all of the disciplines in-house, so being able to communicate efficiently without being physically present was a great skill to practice for future professional use. It helped us learn how to clearly represent our thoughts so that nothing became lost in translation.

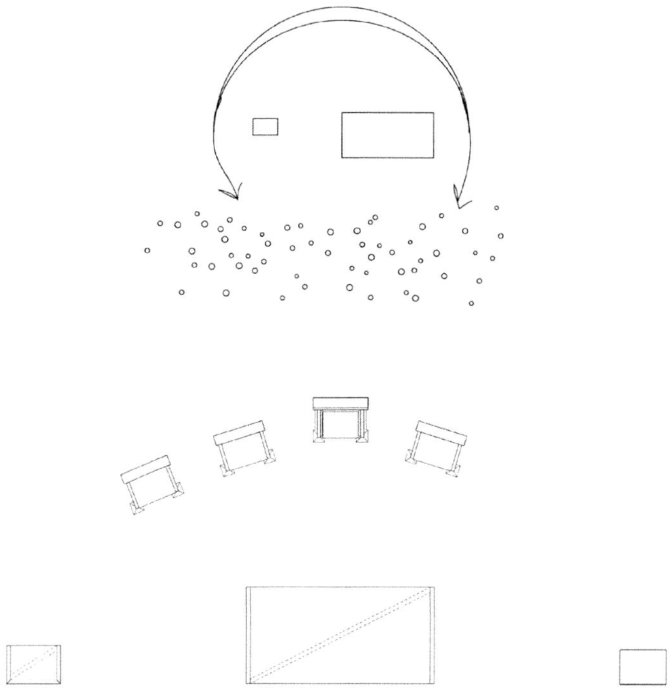

In anticipation of the Pope's upcoming encyclical Laudato Si, this design reflects a kinship between the Church and the environment responsibly in a very simple form. As with Pope Francis' visit, the themes of environmentalism and stewardship guided the design process to create a finished product reflecting his role as the shepherd of Catholics.

Pope Francis' teaching is deeply influenced by Marian theology. Pope Francis, as the shepherd of Catholics, celebrates mass within the simplicity of such pieces, elevating that kinship to a sacramental level. The orientation of the papal and deacon's chairs along a crescent shape face toward the altar show this Marian influence, and reach toward the congregation, embracing them as the People of the Church. Further, this orientation frames the ambo and altar, placing the emphasis on the message of the Church spoken by Pope Francis.

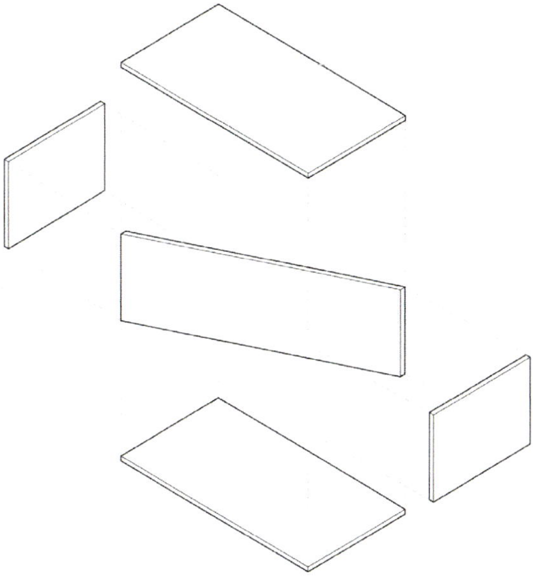

Altar Exploded Axon/Perspective

The wood will be reclaimed from local churches and constructed with environmentally friendly methods to reflect Pope Francis's message. The stone will match the Basilica in order to symbolize the Church and, in the context of Pope Francis's message, will be surrounded by the reclaimed wood. The wood represents the environment and nature's role in the Church community, while the stone symbolizes the stability and tradition of the Church.

Ambo Perspective

Lectern Perspective

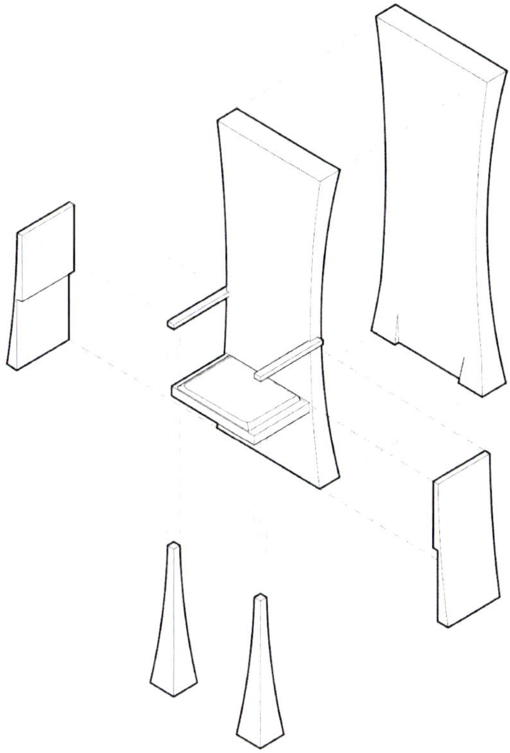

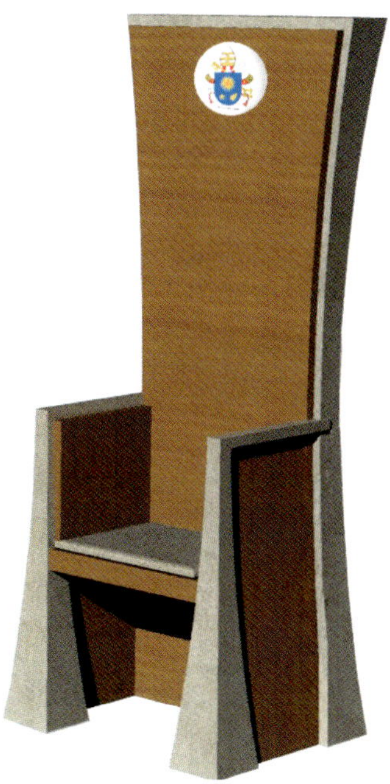

Papal Chair Perspective

Deacon's Chair Perspective

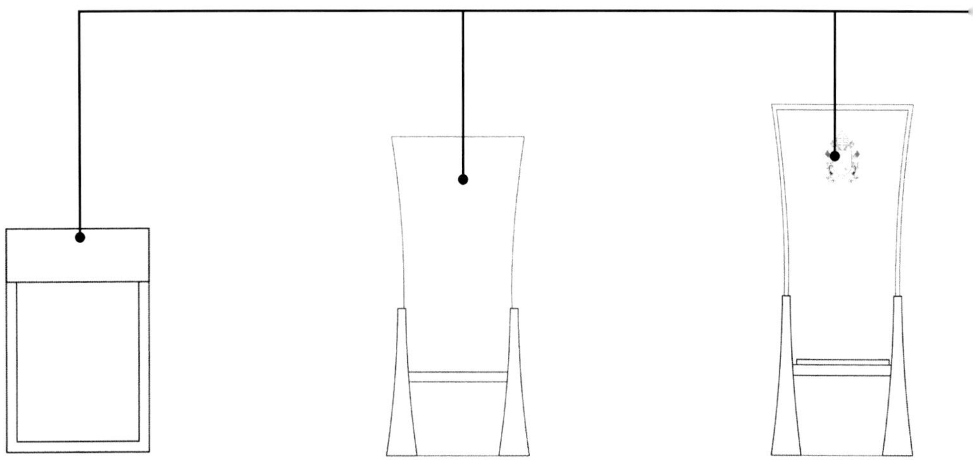

Ambo/Deacon's Chair/Papal Chair Elevation

The ambo, the source of evangelization, will be constructed from relcaimed wood, while the deacons' chairs will be constructed from beige granite. The kinship is simply stated again but will be exquisitly executed, as the beige granite with its veins and complex details is juxtaposed with the darker wood. The papal chair is distinguished by the papal crest, a taller backrest and an upholstered seat.

Beige Granite

Reclaimed Wood

Altar/Lectern Elevation

The pieces are designed to reflect the color of materials extracted from the earth. The most emphasis is upon the ambo and altar; through their form they reveal the Church's emphasized teachings on growth and kinship. The subtle contrast in light on the stone of the altar and on the ambo represents the Church's doctrine rising up to environmental responsibilities and striving for a better community.

HUMBLE BEGINNINGS

Fr. Ugochukwu Nnebue (M. Arch), Megan Gregory (M. Arch), Emily O'Loughlin (M. Arch), Claudia Jean (M. Arch) and Victoria Wallace (M. Arch)

About the Team

We all decided it would be more helpful to have multiple opinions and the maximum number of people working on the project since it was so close to finals week and everyone was busy with other projects. We are all persuing a Master's of Architecture degree with a concentration in Sacred Space. We were friends prior to the competition, and having taken many classes together, were familiar with each other's work and design sense. We knew we could collaborate well to produce a design we all would feel proud of.

The pivotal moment occurred when we decided to strive for simplicity. The Pope's desire for simplicity and back-to-basics mentality helped to push us in a direction where other groups did not go. Our pivotal moment was when we finalized a design idea that we believed was representative of Pope Francis' unique message. It was at this moment that we became unified as a team.

It helps if everyone is in the same area and, even with technology today, it is very hard to stay on the same page with such different schedules. As students, it is easy to become accustomed to designing for oneself, and this competition was an opportunity for us to learn how best to design for someone else. There was critical thought about how design could convey the Pope's teachings, and the challenge was blending what we believed represented these along with one appropriate for the permanent high altar in the Basilica of the National Shrine.

Altar Interior Perspective

Slender, smooth, elegant forms made with stone face represent the serene strength of the Catholic Church, paired with Pope Francis' teachings on dignified humility. The narrow base of the altar signifies the humble beginnings of the Church, Christ and His Twelve Apostles. The altar gently grows wider towards its top, representing the universal reach of Christ's Word.

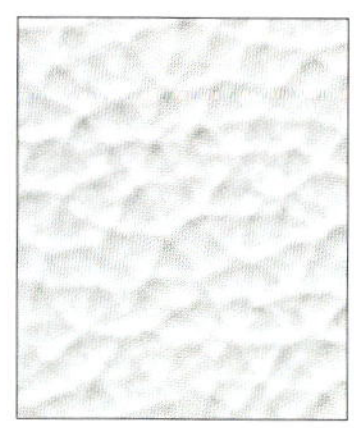

A repetitive design adorns the .75"-thick stone facing which will envelop all pieces of furniture. All pieces are hollow to allow for lightness in weight and thus ease of transportation. As such, the interior framework for the furniture will be wood. The top of the altar is separate from the bottom. The back of the altar includes space for the placement of Saint Junípero Serra's relic, located directly across from the intersection of the arms of the cross on the front of the altar, symbolizing the heart of the mass (see Image 1, pg. 208). Representing the solidity of the faith without extravagance, pieces from a simple wood frame encompassed by marble reflect the humble beginnings of our faith, our Holy Father, and his mission in the Catholic Church.

ALTAR
2
1
POPE'S CHAIR
3
DEACON'S CHAIR
AMBO
CANTOR'S PODIUM

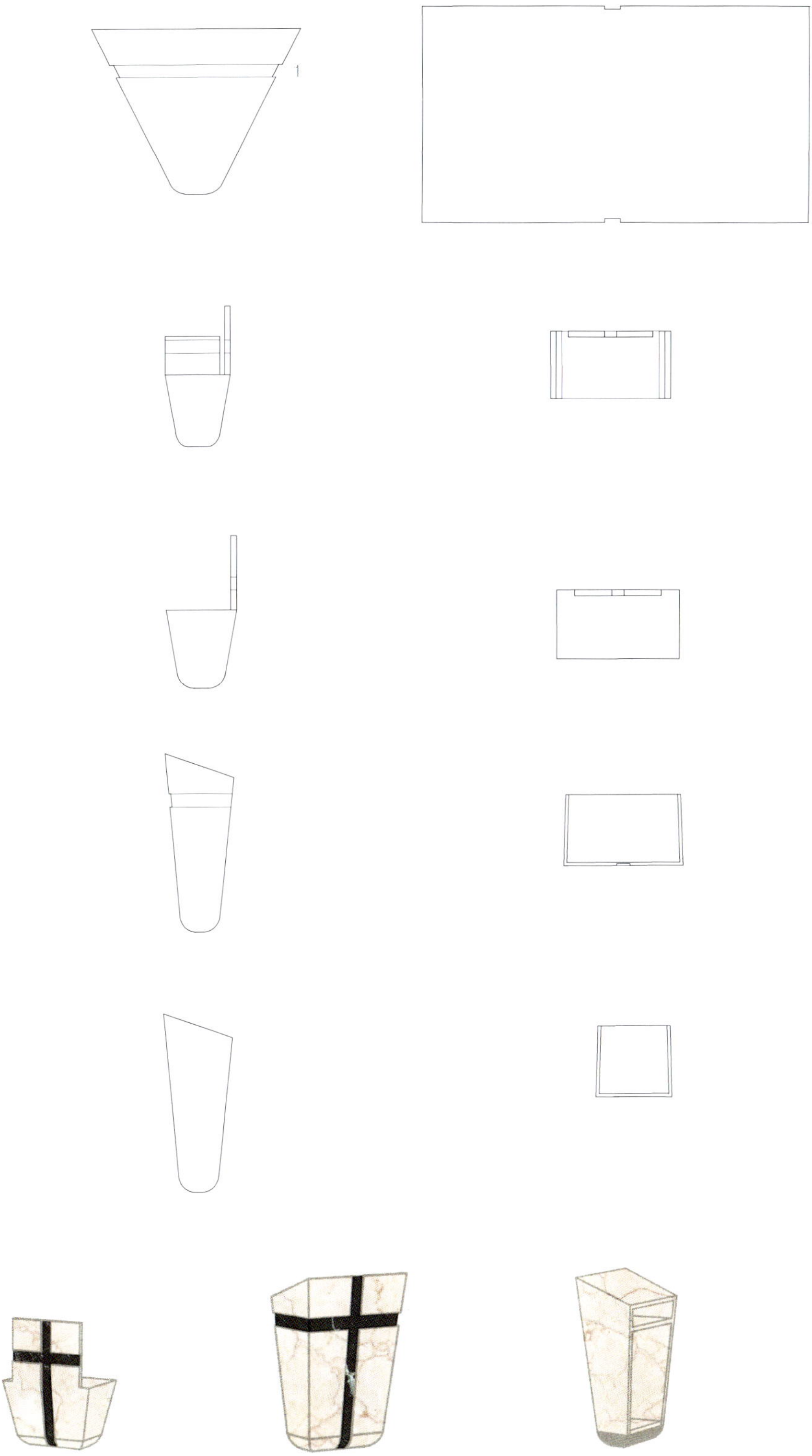
1

THE CANONIZATION OF BL. JUNÍPERO SERRA

Christian Zeitler (B.S. Arch) and John Homer (B.S. Arch)

2nd Place Winner

About the Team

We have been friends since freshman year, and generally see eye to eye on design. When the competition was first announced, we immediately thought of each other.

The design of the chairs was a strong pivot from the Byzantine massing of the altar. We both agreed that they should appear stronger, more in keeping with the remainder. In retrospect, the decision to differentiate them so strongly may have negatively influenced the design in the eyes of the jury.

Design competitions will always have an element of the unknown to them. You can research and strategize until you are blue in the face and still fall short in the end. Ultimately, the best approach is to trust your gut, give it your all, and hope for the best.

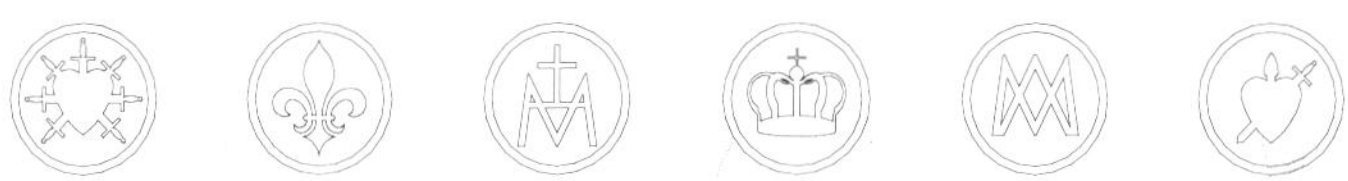

This proposal aims to express a certain American character that permeates local churches. The altar bears iconography that testifies to this American heritage. Ten statues of American saints support the front and back. The sides bear hybrid shields with Marian symbols at their head, evoking both the support of the civic institutions and the intercession of Mary Immaculate, Patroness of the United States.

Altar Elevation

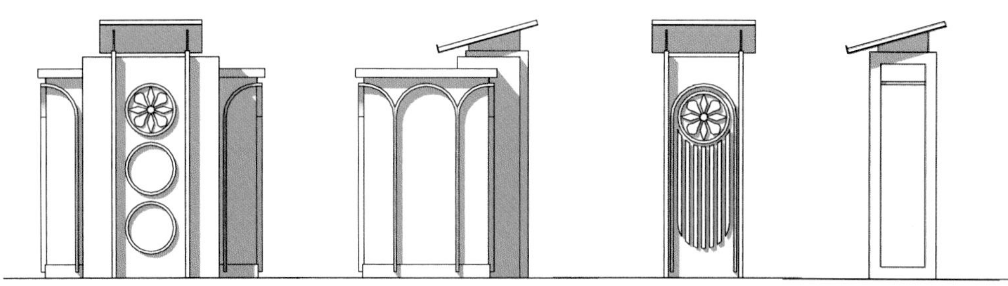

Ambo/Lectern/Deacon's Chair/Papal Chair Elevation

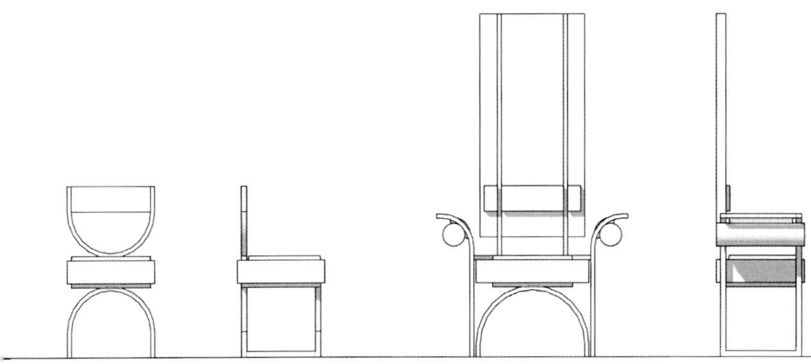

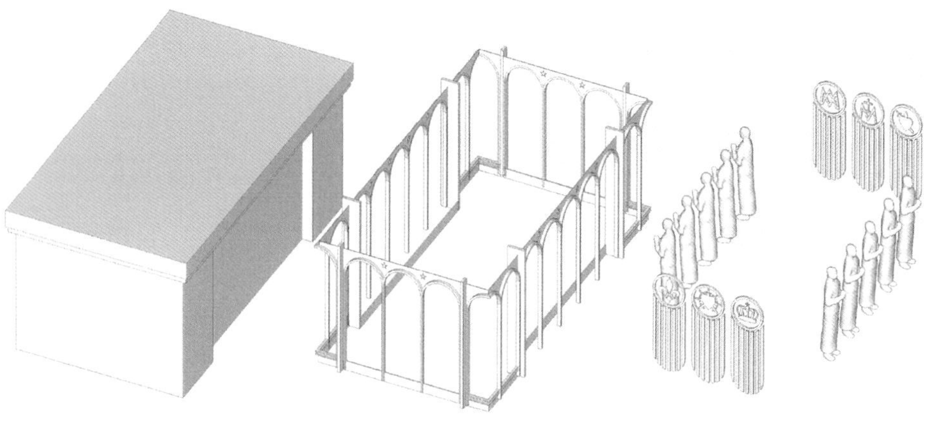

Altar Deconstruct Diagram

Stone dominates the altar and ambo, linking the Gospel and Eucharist through common material. Wood is pronounced more in the seats and ancillary furnishings as the strong Byzantine proportions of the altar gradually give way to a formal architectural expression, and purer in its geometry. Bronze trim, seen also in the Basilica's altar rail and sacristy door, tie the two together in a way that is both timeless and contemporary.

Fabrication will be greatly simplified through the use of digital fabrication techniques and the simplicity of the design's forms. Both the stone and wood will require no complex cuts; engraving on wood will be achieved through a laser cutter. Most metalwork employs simple curves and flush connections. Complex shapes will be cut from sheet metal by a plasma cutter. A truly patriotic design, the reflection of our first American canonization is manifest in these pieces.

Altar Model